Contents

UNIT 13   ADJECTIVES AND ADVERBS

UNIT 14   THE PRESENT PERFECT TENSE

UNIT 8
THE FUTURE TENSE

8a The Future Tense: *Be Going To*
Student Book 1 p. 194, Student Book 1B p. 2

1 Practice

Complete the sentences with the correct form of *be going to*.

1. Jose ___*is going to*___ go to the Philippines next summer.

2. Amy _____ meet him there.

3. They _____ get married.

4. Then they _____ travel to Hawaii.

5. Jose _____ work in Japan.

6. Amy _____ teach English there.

7. They (not) _____ have children right away.

8. They _____ stay in Japan for five years.

9. They (not) _____ buy a house.

10. I _____ visit them next year.

11. I (not) _____ stay very long.

12. They _____ be happy together.

2 Practice

Complete the conversations with *be going to* and the verbs in parentheses.

A. A: What (do) ___*are*___ you ___*going to do*___ this weekend?
                   ₁   (1)
   B: I (not, do) _____ anything. I (stay) _____ in bed, and I
                      2   3
     (sleep) _____ a lot. What (do) _____ you _____?
                4   5   (5)
   A: I (see) _____ a movie. After that, I (eat) _____ Indian food.
              6   7

B. A: Why are you smiling?
   B: I (go) _____ to Paris for four days.
              1
   A: Four days? Why?

B: I (visit) _____ some friends. They (get) _____ married.
2   3

A: That's great!

B: Yes, and I (stay) _____ at their house, and they (buy) _____
4   5

my ticket.

A: You're lucky!

3 | Practice

Write predictions using *be going to* and a phrase from the list. Use contractions when possible.

buy some flowers	have a dinner party	rain
call a friend	not get up	ride her bike
eat his lunch	not take the bus	take a test tomorrow
go on vacation	order a pizza	

1. Patrick has a sandwich.

   He's/Patrick's going to eat his lunch .

2. Sheri is putting on her helmet.

   _____.

3. David is looking at a pizza menu.

   _____.

4. Tim turned off his alarm.

   _____.

5. Carrie is picking up her phone.

   _____.

6. Sue and Carol are taking money out of their wallets.

   _____.

7. Maria is waiting for a taxi and carrying a suitcase.

   _____.

8. Walter is studying.

   _____.

9. Roberto bought a lot of food!

   _____.

10. Min is taking his umbrella.

_____.

11. Sandra is picking up her car keys.

_____.

4 | Practice

Write about what you are going to do or are not going to do on your next vacation.

  1. study

    I'm not going to study on my vacation _____.

  2. wake up early

_____.

  3. take photos

_____.

  4. visit a friend

_____.

  5. send postcards

_____.

  6. swim in the ocean

_____.

  7. read the paper

_____.

  8. leave the country

_____.

  9. email friends

_____.

10. speak English

_____.

5 | Practice

Your friend is going to open a new restaurant. Use the prompts to write questions. Write your own answers.

  1. when/it/open

    When is it going to open _____?

    Next Wednesday _____.

2. what/kind of food/it have

_____?

_____.

3. how many/people/work there

_____?

_____.

4. where/it/be

_____?

_____.

5. what/waiters/wear

_____?

_____.

6. when/you/quit/your job

_____?

_____.

8b Future Time Expressions

Student Book 1 p. 199, Student Book 1B p. 7

6 Practice

Write about your future plans. Use time expressions and _be going to_.

1. Next winter, _____.

2. In a couple years, _____.

3. In 15 minutes, _____.

4. A week from today, _____.

5. Next weekend, _____.

6. Tomorrow morning, _____.

7. Tonight, _____.

8. In three weeks, _____ .

9. In two hours, _____ .

10. After school next Monday, _____ .

7 Practice

Complete the following sentences. Use *tomorrow, next, in, yesterday, last,* and *ago*.

1. Renata and Claudia met six years _____ *ago* _____ .

Now, they go on vacation together.

2. _____ year, they went to Bali.

3. _____ , they left for Mexico.

4. _____ , they are going to go to the beach.

5. _____ five days, they're going to visit

Mexico City.

6. _____ week, they're going to take a tour.

7. They're going to come back _____ two weeks.

8. They decided to go on this trip three months _____ .

9. _____ month, they bought their tickets.

8 Practice

Write *C* beside the sentence if *tomorrow, next, in, yesterday, last,* or *ago* are used correctly. Write *I* if *tomorrow, next, in, yesterday, last,* or *ago* are used incorrectly.

___*I*___ **1.** They got married next week.

_____ **2.** Karina is going to take her driver's test two days ago.

_____ **3.** We're going to the museum tomorrow.

_____ **4.** What did you do in 10 minutes ago?

_____ **5.** Where is he going to be yesterday?

_____ **6.** Ronaldo didn't come with us last week.

_____ **7.** Four years ago, Deborah was living in Atlanta.

_____ **8.** Yutaka is going to study art next semester.

_____ **9.** In 30 minutes, class is going to finish.

_____ **10.** A week ago, I'm going to move to a new apartment.

8c The Future Tense: The Present Progressive as a Future Tense

Student Book 1 p. 201, Student Book 1B p. 9

9 Practice

A. Andy is going to college. Write about what he is doing this Thursday. Write sentences using the present progressive for the future.

Time	Activity
9:00	arrive at dorm
9:30	meet roommate
9:30 – 10:00	put clothes away
12:00 – 1:00	have lunch with other students
1:00 – 2:00	tour campus
2:00 – 3:00	meet with advisor
3:00 – 4:00	choose classes
5:00	go back to dorm
5:30 – 6:30	talk with roommate
6:30 – 7:30	eat dinner
8:30 – 11:30	attend welcome party

1. 9:00   _Andy is arriving at his dorm at 9:00_ .

2. 5:00   _____ .

3. 12:00 – 1:00 _____ .

4. 3:00 – 4:00 _____ .

5. 8:30 – 11:30 _____ .

6. 9:30 _____ .

7. 6:30 – 7:30 _____ .

8. 9:30 – 10:00 _____ .

9. 2:00 – 3:00 _____ .

10. 5:30 – 6:30 _____ .

11. 1:00 – 2:00 _____ .

B. Write questions and answers about Andy's schedule.

1. what/time/arrive/at dorm

   <u>What time is Andy arriving at the dorm</u> _____ ?

   <u>He's arriving at 9:00</u> _____ .

2. who/he/meet/at 9:30

   _____

   _____

3. who/he/have/lunch with

   _____

   _____

4. when/he/choose classes

   _____

   _____

5. what/he/do/5:30

   _____

   _____

6. when/he/go back/to dorm

   _____

   _____

10 Practice

Complete the conversations using the present progressive as a future tense.

A. A: When's your last class?

B: I (take) _____<u>'m taking</u>_____ my last test tomorrow at 10:00. Then I
                           1

(come) _____ back home and (pack) _____
          2   3

my suitcase. I (catch) _____ a plane at 1:00.
                                4

B. A: What (do) _____ you _____ this summer?
                             1   **(1)**

  B: I (go) _____ on vacation with my family for two weeks. Then for
                         2

      six weeks I (work) _____ part time at my uncle's pizza restaurant.
                                   3

      He (go) _____ to Italy. In August, I (hike)
                      4

      _____ for ten days in national parks with my brother.
              5

  B: That sounds great.

  A: What about you?

  B: I (take) _____ two classes in Chicago this summer. I (stay)
                       6

      _____ with my aunt, and I (not, live) _____ in
           7   **8**

      the dorm.

  A: How (get) _____ you _____ there?
                       9   **(9)**

  B: I (fly) _____.
                  10

II Practice

Write *F* if the statement is in the future. Write *N* if the statement is happening now.

_____ **1.** I'm going home in two days.

_____ **2.** We're having a good time.

_____ **3.** She's leaving tomorrow.

_____ **4.** The children are making cookies Saturday morning.

_____ **5.** Our class is having a test next week.

_____ **6.** We're not sleeping right now.

_____ **7.** He isn't working at the moment.

_____ **8.** Mark and Eileen are working on the computer.

_____ **9.** Julia and Miguel are going out tonight.

_____ **10.** Are you coming back soon?

8d The Future Tense: *Will*

Student Book 1 p. 205, Student Book 1B p. 13

12 Practice

Make predictions for the year 2100. Use *will* or *won't* to complete the sentences.

1. People _____*will*_____ have disposable clothes.

2. Women _____ shave their heads.

3. People _____ read newspapers.

4. Men _____ wear make up.

5. Cars _____ use gas.

6. Students _____ attend school from home.

7. English _____ disappear.

8. People _____ have homes underwater.

9. Everyone _____ look the same.

10. Men and women _____ need to sleep.

11. People _____ communicate without speaking.

13 Practice

Complete the conversations with the future tense. Use forms of the present progressive, *will*, or *be going to*.

A. Stefan: I (get) _____ lunch right now. Do you want anything?
   ₁

   Adam: Sure. I (have) _____ a cheese sandwich, or maybe some
   ₂

   soup. What (get) _____ you _____?
   ₃   ₍₃₎

   Stefan: I (think) _____ about pizza.
   ₄

   Adam: Oh, that sounds good. I (have) _____ pizza too.
   ₅

B. Sandra: I don't feel well.

   Gerald: That's okay. I (make) _____ dinner.
   ₁

C. Jackie: I (go) _____ home in a few minutes.
   ₁

   Eric: Okay. I (see) _____ you tomorrow.
   ₂

D. Ginny: What (do) _____ you _____ tomorrow
                                                 1   (1)

             night?

    Ed: I (go) _____ to bed early.
                              2

    Ginny: I (rent) _____ a movie. Do you want to come over? I
                              3

          (pick) _____ you up, and I (take) _____ you home.
                      4   5

    Ed: No, thanks. I'm really tired.

E. Sachiko: Where (be) _____ you _____ this time
                              1   (1)

             next year?

    Marcela: I don't know. Maybe I (be) _____ in San Diego, or maybe I
                                            2

          (move) _____ to Houston.
                            3

F. Announcer: The concert (start) _____ at 3:00, but the doors
                                      1

          (open) _____ at 2:30. Three bands (play)
                            2

          _____. There (be) _____ a short
                  3   4

          break at 5:00. The concert (finish) _____ about 7:00.
                                          5

G. Kathy: I really don't understand this exercise.

    Sam: I do. I (help) _____ you. I (study) _____
                            1   2

          tonight at about 7:00.

    Kathy: Oh, thanks. I (call) _____ you then.
                                  3

H. Romero: What (do) _____ you
                              1

             _____ now?
                  (1)

    Beth: Nothing. Why?

    Romero: Dean, Elizabeth, and I (go) _____
                                        2

          the park in an hour. Do you want to come with us?

    Beth: Sure. Oh, I (get) _____ another call.
                                  3

          I (call) _____ you right back.
                          4

    Romero: Okay, I (talk) _____ to you later.
                              5

8e *May, Might,* and *Will*

Student Book 1 p. 209, Student Book 1B p. 17

14 Practice

Complete the conversations using *will* when the speaker is sure. Use *may* or *might* if the speaker is not sure.

A. Kevin: Carolina, you are from Quebec, right? I

_____ go to Ottawa or Quebec this time
₁

next year. I'm not sure. Is the weather good then?

Carolina: It _____ be. Sometimes it's warm,
₂

sometimes it's cool.

Kevin: I _____ take the train, or I
₃

_____ fly. I don't know now.
₄

Carolina: Do you have a hotel? You _____ need a
₅

reservation. It's very busy this time of year.

Kevin: Okay, I _____ make one tomorrow.
₆

Carolina: And you (not) _____ have any language problems. Everyone
₇

speaks English.

Kevin: That's good.

Carolina: What _____ you do there?
₈

Kevin: I _____ visit museums, or I _____ take a tour.
₉ ₁₀

Carolina: I'm sure you _____ have a good time!
₁₁

B. Patty: _____ I have a drink of water?
₁

Larry: Sure.

C. Michi: This is a nice restaurant. What are you going to have?

Paula: I don't know. I _____ have fish, or I _____ have tofu.
₁ ₂

Michi: I think the fish sounds good.

Waiter: Are you ready to order?

Michi: Yes, I _____ have the fish.
                        3

Paula: And I _____ have the tofu.
                      4

Waiter: Anything to drink?

Michi: I _____ have some water, please.
                    5

Paula: Me, too.

15 Practice

Underline the correct verbs in parentheses.

1. I (might go / am going) to the doctor's tomorrow. I have an appointment.

2. I (might shop / am shopping). I don't know now.

3. I (might meet / am meeting) a friend for lunch. We have a reservation at 1:00.

4. We (might go / are going to go) to a movie. We bought our tickets yesterday.

5. She (might come / is coming) to my house later. I don't know now.

6. I ('ll be / might be) home at 6:00. We eat dinner then.

7. My husband (will read / might read) the children a story. Sometimes I do it.

8. The children (will go / might go) to bed at 9:00 because it's their bedtime.

9. My husband and I (are going to watch / might watch) a movie. I don't know now.

10. We (will go / might go) to bed around 11:30. We never stay up late.

16 Practice

Write five things you may or might do next weekend. Use ideas from the list or your own.

| eat at a restaurant | go to the gym | shop | visit the library |
| go to a museum | meet friends | stay home | watch TV |

1. _I might shop this Saturday_____.

2. _____.

3. _____.

4. _____ .

5. _____ .

6. _____ .

8f Future Time Clauses with *Before*, *After*, and *When*

Student Book 1 p. 212, Student Book 1B p. 20

17 Practice

Joe is going back to Virginia for summer vacation. Underline the time clauses in the sentences about him.

1. Before he goes home, he'll finish his classes.

2. After he finishes school, he'll buy a ticket to Virginia.

3. Joe will be happy when he goes home.

4. When his parents see him, they will hug him.

5. After he gets home, his friends will call him.

6. He'll see a lot of movies when he's there.

7. After he gets home, he'll get a part-time job.

8. He'll email his friends before he comes back to Los Angeles.

9. Joe is going to ask his girlfriend to visit him before he leaves Virginia.

10. When he arrives, his friends will be at the airport to meet him.

18 Practice

Complete the conversations with the verbs in parentheses. Remember that future time clauses use the simple present tense in the time clause and the future tense in the main clause.

A. Tony: When you (get) _____ to the party, I
                                              1

(introduce) _____ you to Sophie. She's nice. You
                            2

(like) _____ her. Before you (meet) _____
                3   4

her, I (tell) _____ her about you.
                          5

Chris: Okay, thanks. Before I (leave) _____ my house, I
6

(call) _____ you.
7

Tony: I think everyone (be) _____ here when you
8

(arrive) _____. Do you have the CDs?
9

Chris: Yes, I (give) _____ them to you when I
10

(see) _____ you.
11

B. Donna: How do I get to your house?

Cesar: First, go down Main Street. When you (come) _____ to the
1

corner, you (see) _____ the library. Turn right. After you
2

(go) _____ two blocks, you (see) _____
3   4

my house.

Donna: Okay. I (be) _____ there in a few minutes.
5

C. After I (finish) _____ school, I (take) _____
1   2

a trip to Europe. I (see) _____ France, Italy, Spain, Germany,
3

Hungary, and the Czech Republic. After I (return) _____, I
4

(look) _____ for a job. When I (find) _____
5   6

a good one, I (make) _____ some money. After I
7

(save) _____ some money, I (buy) _____ a
8   9

small house. I (have) _____ a big garden in the back yard. I
10

(have) _____ dinner parties every weekend.
11

19 Practice
Answer the questions.

1. What are you going to do after you finish this exercise?

_____.

2. What are you going to do before you go to bed tonight?

_____.

3. What are you going to tell your teacher when you go to your next class?

_____.

8g Future Conditional Sentences

Student Book 1 p. 215, Student Book 1B p. 23

20 Practice

Match the sentence parts. Then write the sentences.

_d_	**1.** go to college	**a.** eyes get tired
_____	**2.** drink a lot of coffee	**b.** not feel healthy
_____	**3.** finish homework	**c.** have time for parties
_____	**4.** wear a helmet	**d.** get a good job
_____	**5.** work a long time at the computer	**e.** not be late to work
_____	**6.** find a part time job	**f.** not sleep
_____	**7.** get up early	**g.** make a little money
_____	**8.** not exercise	**h.** be safe on a bicycle
_____	**9.** not brush teeth	**i.** not have any teeth left

1. _If you go to college, you'll get a good job_____.

2. _____.

3. _____.

4. _____.

5. _____.

6. _____.

7. _____.

8. _____.

9. _____.

21 **Practice**

Complete the sentences with the correct form of the verbs in parentheses. Sometimes two answers are possible.

1. We (go) _____ to Brazil on our next vacation if we

   (get) _____ cheap tickets.

2. If we (visit) _____ the beaches in Rio, we

   (not, have) _____ to go to the Amazon.

3. If we (go) _____ to the Amazon, we (visit) _____

   our friends there.

4. If they (have) _____ time, they (join) _____

   us on a tour of the Amazon River.

5. We (stay) _____ with our friends, or we (stay) _____

   in a hotel. We don't know now.

6. If we (stay) _____ in a hotel, we (eat) _____

   at restaurants.

7. If we (stay) _____ with our friends, we (have)

   _____ meals with them.

8. If we (not, go) _____ to the Amazon, we (stay)

   _____ in Rio.

9. If we (stay) _____ in Rio, we (visit) _____ Sao Paulo.

10. If we (have) _____ a good time in Brazil, we (come)

    _____ back next year.

8h The Simple Present Tense with Time Clauses and *If* Clauses

Student Book 1 p. 218, Student Book 1B p. 26

22 Practice

Match the sentence parts. Then write the sentences using *when, before, after,* or *if* in the time clause.

_b_ **1.** When you water plants,

_____ **2.** Before the sun comes up every morning,

_____ **3.** After lunch,

_____ **4.** If you don't open the windows,

_____ **5.** When I go to the café,

_____ **6.** After it rains,

a. I usually buy a sandwich.

b. they grow.

c. the river's water rises.

d. Tom always drinks coffee.

e. I go for a three-mile run.

f. the apartment will be too hot.

1. _When you water plants, they grow_ _____.

2. _____.

3. _____.

4. _____.

5. _____.

6. _____.

23 Practice

Complete the sentences with main clauses about yourself.

1. If I read the newspaper every morning, _I know what is happening_ ____.

2. If I work out, _____.

3. If I don't do my homework, _____.

4. If I don't eat breakfast, _____.

5. If I work hard, _____.

6. If I don't feel well, _____.

7. When I cook, _____.

8. When I'm lonely, _____.

9. When I'm tired, _____.

10. When I have a problem, _____.

Practice

Complete the sentences with the correct form of the verbs in parentheses.

1. Ryan has class from 10:00 until 3:00 on Monday and Wednesday. After he

(finish) _____ class, he usually (go) _____ to

his part-time job.

2. If he (finish) _____ work early, he (meet) _____

his roommate Tom in the library.

3. This Tuesday, if he (get) _____ up early, he and Tom

(run) _____ for half an hour.

4. After he (run) _____, he (take) _____ a shower.

5. If he (have) _____ a lot of homework this week, he

(study) _____ at home.

6. When he (get) _____ hungry, he usually

(make) _____ a sandwich.

7. This Friday, he and his roommate (have) _____ a party.

8. A lot of people (come) _____.

9. When they (have) _____ parties, Ryan

(make) _____ pizza.

10. If Ryan (not, make) _____ pizza for this party, he

(buy) _____ some other food.

11. If they (not, have) _____ any food, everyone

(be) _____ hungry.

12. Before everyone (arrive) _____, Ryan and Tom

(clean) _____ their apartment.

13. After everyone (leave) _____, they (clean) _____

their apartment again!

14. If the party (go) _____ late, they

(not, get up) _____ early on Saturday.

25 Practice

Answer the questions.

1. What are you going to do if you have some time this weekend?

_____.

2. What do you do when it rains on Saturday?

_____.

3. How do you feel when you do well in your English class?

_____.

4. When you go shopping, what do you usually buy?

_____.

5. When you don't understand the teacher, what do you do?

_____.

6. If you have time today, what are you going to do for fun?

_____.

7. When you finish this exercise, what are you going to do?

_____.

8. What will you do if you don't have any homework tomorrow?

_____.

SELF-TEST

A **Choose the best answer, A, B, C, or D, to complete the sentence. Mark your answer by darkening the oval with the same letter.**

1. Cecile is leaving for New York _____ two hours.

   A. last   Ⓐ Ⓑ Ⓒ Ⓓ
   B. in
   C. next
   D. ago

2. Bob was in the hospital _____ week.

   A. last   Ⓐ Ⓑ Ⓒ Ⓓ
   B. in
   C. next
   D. ago

3. Tina bought the tickets to Hawaii three months _____.

   A. last   Ⓐ Ⓑ Ⓒ Ⓓ
   B. in
   C. next
   D. ago

4. Kelly will call you when she _____ her work.

   A. is finishing   Ⓐ Ⓑ Ⓒ Ⓓ
   B. finishes
   C. will finish
   D. is going to finish

5. When I _____ TV, I usually go to sleep.

   A. will watch   Ⓐ Ⓑ Ⓒ Ⓓ
   B. might watch
   C. watched
   D. watch

6. _____ you have a headache, take some aspirin.

   A. If   Ⓐ Ⓑ Ⓒ Ⓓ
   B. Might
   C. Will
   D. May

7. When Mimi sees her son, she _____ be so happy.

   A. is   Ⓐ Ⓑ Ⓒ Ⓓ
   B. is being
   C. is going to
   D. will

8. D. J. _____ a computer class this weekend.

   A. might   Ⓐ Ⓑ Ⓒ Ⓓ
   B. will
   C. takes
   D. is taking

9. What _____ at 12:00 today?

   A. will you   Ⓐ Ⓑ Ⓒ Ⓓ
   B. do you
   C. are you doing
   D. are you do

10. After Peg _____ up, she has two cups of coffee.

    A. gets   Ⓐ Ⓑ Ⓒ Ⓓ
    B. will get
    C. is getting
    D. is going to get

B   Find the underlined word or phrase, A, B, C, or D, that is incorrect. Mark your answer by darkening the oval with the same letter.

1. Where <u>were you</u> <u>staying</u> <u>last week</u> <u>ago</u>?
        A   B   C   D

   Ⓐ Ⓑ Ⓒ Ⓓ

2. <u>We're</u> <u>going to</u> be married <u>last</u> <u>six months</u>.
     A   B   C   D

   Ⓐ Ⓑ Ⓒ Ⓓ

3. <u>She'll have</u> breakfast <u>before</u> she <u>will leave</u>
      A   B   C

   for <u>work</u>.
       D

   Ⓐ Ⓑ Ⓒ Ⓓ

4. <u>If he</u> <u>is going to get</u> the job, he <u>will buy</u>
    A   B   C

   <u>a new laptop</u>.
       D

   Ⓐ Ⓑ Ⓒ Ⓓ

5. <u>I'm going to</u> <u>have</u> dinner <u>in two hours</u> <u>ago</u>.
      A   B   C   D

   Ⓐ Ⓑ Ⓒ Ⓓ

6. <u>If Todd has</u> <u>a lot of work</u>, he <u>stays</u> late
      A   B   C

   <u>at work</u> tomorrow.
     D

   Ⓐ Ⓑ Ⓒ Ⓓ

7. Amada <u>is going</u> <u>to go</u> to Athens on her
          A   B

   <u>last</u> <u>vacation</u>.
    C   D

   Ⓐ Ⓑ Ⓒ Ⓓ

8. <u>Yesterday</u>, <u>John is</u> going to <u>start</u>
      A   B   C

   <u>his new job</u>.
      D

   Ⓐ Ⓑ Ⓒ Ⓓ

9. I <u>might</u> <u>not go</u> to the <u>party</u> <u>with you</u>
      A   B   C   D

   tonight.

   Ⓐ Ⓑ Ⓒ Ⓓ

10. <u>If they</u> <u>will have</u> time, <u>they'll come</u>
     A   B   C

   <u>to the party</u> with us.
       D

   Ⓐ Ⓑ Ⓒ Ⓓ

UNIT 9
QUANTITY AND DEGREE WORDS

9a *All Of, Almost All Of, Most Of,* and *Some Of*
Student Book 1 p. 226, Student Book 1B p. 34

1 Practice
Look at the picture and complete the sentences with *all of, almost all of, most of,* or *some of.*

1. _____Some of_____ the people are children.

2. _____ the people are adults.

3. _____ the adults are men.

4. _____ the adults are dressed up.

5. _____ the adults are eating and drinking.

6. _____ the adults are talking.

7. _____ the adults are playing cards.

8. _____ the children are playing.

2 Practice
Look at the photo and complete the sentences with *all of, almost all of, most of,* or *some of.*

1. _____ the students are wearing jeans.

2. _____ the people are students.

3. _____ the people are men.

4. _____ the people are women.

5. _____ the people have dark hair.

6. _____ the students are paying attention.

7. _____ the students are looking at the teacher.

3 Practice

Look at the photo and complete the sentences with *all of, almost all of, most of,* or *some of.*

1. _____ the people are in an elevator.

2. _____ the people are worried.

3. _____ the people are men.

4. _____ the people are women.

5. _____ the people are wearing suits.

4 Practice

Read about Courtney's birthday party. Circle the correct verb.

1. All of the presents (is / are) wonderful.

2. Some of the music (is / are) good.

3. Almost all of the people (is / are) dancing.

4. Some of the balloons (is / are) on the floor.

5. All of the food (is / are) delicious.

6. Some of the people (is / are) talking.

5 Practice

Read about the new supermarket. Circle the correct verb.

1. All of the vegetables (is / are) fresh.

2. Some of the fruit (is / are) from South America.

3. All of the customers (is / are) happy.

4. Most of the cashiers (is / are) new.

5. Most of the coffee (is / are) cheap.

6. Some of the wines (is / are) expensive.

7. Almost all of the cheese (is / are) tasty.

8. All of the shelves (is / are) clean.

9. Some of the bread (is / are) delicious.

10. Almost all of the flowers (is / are) beautiful.

6 Practice

Write about the people on your street. Use *all of, almost all of, most of,* or *some of.*

1. _____ work.
2. _____ wear suits.
3. _____ ride bicycles.
4. _____ drive every day.
5. _____ have children.
6. _____ have pets.
7. _____ are nice.
8. _____ are married.
9. _____ travel a lot.
10. _____ smoke.

9b *Every*

Student Book 1 p. 229, Student Book 1B p. 37

7 Practice

Rewrite each sentence using *every*.

1. All of the computers work.

   _____.

2. All of the students in this school are studying English.

   _____.

3. All of the chairs are comfortable.

   _____.

4. All of the flowers smell good.

   _____.

5. All of the photographs are funny.

   _____.

6. All of the Japanese restaurants are delicious.

   _____.

7. All the neighbors are nice.

   _____.

8. All of the birds are singing.

   _____.

9. All of the students are laughing.

_____ .

10. All of the exercises are interesting.

_____ .

8 Practice

Write _C_ next to the sentence if _every_ or _all_ is used correctly. Write _I_ if _every_ or _all_ is used incorrectly.

_____ **1.** Every students have a dictionary.

_____ **2.** All the students are intelligent.

_____ **3.** Every star is out tonight.

_____ **4.** All the window is open.

_____ **5.** Every cell phone is off.

_____ **6.** Every waiters are wearing white.

_____ **7.** All the shoes are dirty.

_____ **8.** All the book is good.

_____ **9.** Every house on our street is big.

_____ **10.** All the players is good.

9c _Very_ and _Too_

Student Book 1 p. 231, Student Book 1B p. 39

9 Practice

Answer the questions. Use _too_ or _very_ and adjectives from the list.

cold	short
difficult	tired
noisy	young

1. Why can't she sleep? _____ .

2. Why is he working so hard on the exercise? _____ .

3. Why can't she drive? _____ .

4. Why can't she reach the top shelf? _____.

5. Why is he staying home tonight? _____.

6. Why is she wearing a jacket? _____.

10 Practice

Match the sentence parts.

_____ **1.** The music is too loud.

_____ **2.** Chad is very sick.

_____ **3.** Mimi is very smart.

_____ **4.** This exam is too hard.

_____ **5.** She's a very good photographer.

_____ **6.** I'm too busy.

_____ **7.** The suitcase is very heavy.

_____ **8.** I'm very tired.

a. I'm going to take a nap.

b. Her photos are wonderful.

c. He needs to see a doctor.

d. I won't pass it.

e. I can't go with you.

f. I can't pick it up.

g. She always does well in school.

h. I can't study.

11 Practice

Complete the sentences with *too* or *very* and adjectives from the list.

angry	excited	hot	sour
cheap	far	large	thin
cold	happy	late	thirsty
difficult	high	nice	

1. You can't eat that lemon. It's _too sour_____.

2. I'm going to buy that car. It's _____.

3. I need some water. I'm _____.

4. I like Rita. She's _____.

5. I'm going to put on a jacket. I'm _____.

6. I don't want to walk. It's _____.

7. Tom can't drink the coffee. It's _____.

8. I'm getting married! I'm _____.

9. You've lost a lot of weight. You're _____.

10. I don't understand the exercise. It's _____.

11. Sue missed her bus. She got up _____.

12. Phil didn't buy that jacket. It's _____.

13. I can't sleep. I'm _____.

14. Mrs. Brown won't talk to anyone. She's _____.

15. I can't reach the shelf. It's _____.

12 Practice

Choose the answer that describes you. Circle *a* or *b*.

1. Do you like to ski?
   a. No, it's too cold.
   b. Yes, but it's very cold.

2. Can you go out on the weekend?
   a. No, I'm too busy.
   b. Yes, but I'm busy.

3. Do you understand science?
   a. No, it's too difficult.
   b. Yes, but sometimes it's very difficult.

4. Do you like cake?
   a. No, it's too sweet.
   b. Yes, but it's very sweet.

5. Do you like to get up early?
   a. No, I'm usually too tired.
   b. Yes, but I'm very tired.

9d *Too Many* and *Too Much*

Student Book 1 p. 234, Student Book 1B p. 42

13 Practice

Complete the sentences about class problems with *too much* or *too many*.

1. There are _____*too many*_____ students.

2. There are _____ exercises.

3. There is _____ homework.

4. There is _____ information.

5. There are _____ books.

6. There is _____ noise.

14 **Practice**

Complete the sentences about a soccer game with *too much* or *too many*.

1. There were _____ people.

2. Jesse ate _____ candy.

3. There was _____ sun and _____ wind.

4. The game took _____ time.

5. One team had _____ players.

6. The other team made _____ mistakes.

15 **Practice**

Dominic and Julia are discussing a movie. Complete their conversation with *too much* or *too many*.

Dominic: Did you like the movie?

Julia: Not really. There was _____ violence.
 1

Dominic: Yes, there were also _____ people there.
 2

Julia: I ate _____ popcorn.
 3

Dominic: Me, too. And, the tickets cost _____ money.
 4

Julia: Driving to the theater was difficult. There was _____ traffic.
 5

16 **Practice**

Write *C* next to the sentence if *too much* or *too many* is used correctly. Write *I* if *too much* or *too many* is used incorrectly.

___C___ 1. The teachers have too much work.

___I___ 2. There's too many noise in the city.

_____ 3. I always have too many homework.

_____ 4. There are too many people at the beach.

_____ 5. We ate too much food.

_____ 6. There is too many crime.

_____ 7. That's too much information.

_____ 8. I have too many exercises.

_____ 9. Becky made too much mistakes.

_____ 10. They have too much problems.

27

Quantity and Degree Words

9e *Too* + Adjective + Infinitive;
Too + Adjective + *For* + Noun/Pronoun + Infinitive

Student Book 1 p. 236, Student Book 1B p. 44

17 ## Practice

**Rewrite the two sentences as one sentence with the same meaning.
Use the "*too* + adjective + infinitive" pattern.**

1. This exercise is difficult. I can't do it.

   This exercise is too difficult to do   .

2. That watch is expensive. I can't buy it.

   _____ .

3. Ray and Norm are worried. They can't sleep.

   _____ .

4. My mother is sleepy. She can't watch TV.

   _____ .

5. Lee is sad. He can't smile.

   _____ .

6. The park is far. We can't walk there from here.

   _____ .

7. They were sick. They couldn't finish their dinner.

   _____ .

8. My daughters are young. They can't go to college.

   _____ .

9. He was busy. He couldn't enjoy his free time.

   _____ .

10. They got up late. They couldn't catch their plane.

    _____ .

18 **Practice**

Linda and Sam went on vacation, but they didn't have a good time. Rewrite the two sentences as one sentence with the same meaning. Use the "*too* + adjective + *for* + noun/pronoun + infinitive" pattern.

1. The weather was hot. Linda couldn't stay on the beach.

   The weather was too hot for Linda to stay on the beach .

2. It was rainy. They couldn't go shopping.

   _____ .

3. The wakeup calls were early. He couldn't get up.

   _____ .

4. The pool was cold. They couldn't get in.

   _____ .

5. The water at the beach was rough. She couldn't swim in it.

   _____ .

6. The hotel rooms were small. They couldn't feel comfortable.

   _____ .

7. The bed was soft. Sam couldn't sleep in it.

   _____ .

8. The bathroom was dirty. She couldn't shower in it.

   _____ .

9. The people in the hotel were unfriendly. He couldn't talk to them.

   _____ .

10. People spoke fast. He couldn't understand them.

_____.

11. The food was spicy. She couldn't eat it.

_____.

12. Linda's bathing suit was large. She couldn't wear it.

_____.

9f ◆ Adjective + *Enough*

Student Book 1 p. 238, Student Book 1B p. 46

19 Practice

Norman doesn't like his hotel. Write sentences using *too* and *enough* and the adjectives in parentheses.

1. The water in the shower (cold). It's not (warm).

   _The water is too cold. It's not warm enough_____.

2. The bed is (hard). It isn't (soft).

   _____.

3. The view is (ugly). It's not (nice).

   _____.

4. The carpet is (dirty). It isn't (clean).

   _____.

5. The restaurant is (crowded). It's not (empty).

   _____.

Linda doesn't like her class or her classroom. Write sentences using *too* and *enough* and the adjectives in parentheses.

6. The room is (cold). It isn't (hot).

   _____.

7. The room is (dark). It isn't (light).

   _____.

8. The desks are (small). They aren't (big).

   _____.

9. The class starts (early). It doesn't start (late).

_____.

10. The tests are (difficult). They're not (easy).

_____.

11. The class is (long). It's not (short).

_____.

12. The subject is (boring). It isn't (interesting).

_____.

Virginia and Maureen are trying on clothes. Maureen doesn't like the jacket. Write sentences using _too_ and _enough_ and the adjectives in parentheses.

13. This jacket is (small). It's not (large).

_____.

14. It's (expensive). It isn't (cheap).

_____.

15. The arms are (short). They aren't (long).

_____.

16. The color is (dark). It isn't (light).

_____.

17. It's (heavy). It isn't (light).

_____.

Cathy doesn't like the city. Write sentences using *too* and *enough* and the adjectives in parentheses.

18. The city is (noisy). It isn't (quiet).

_____.

19. The streets are (crowded). They're not (quiet).

_____.

20. The people are (busy). They aren't (relaxed).

_____.

21. The city is (big). It's not (small).

_____.

22. It's (dangerous). It isn't (safe).

_____.

9g *Enough* + Noun

Student Book 1 p. 240, Student Book 1B p. 48

20 Practice

Complete the sentences with *enough* + a noun from the list.

classes	paint	soap
coffee	police officers	sugar
customers	reservations	time
money	room in the car	water

1. A: Did you finish the test this morning?

   B: No, _I didn't have enough time_ _____.

2. A: Did you buy gas for the car yesterday?

   B: No, _____.

3. A: Did the restaurant close last week?

   B: Yes, _____.

4. A: Did Ivan graduate in June?

   B: No, _____.

5. A: Was the flight cancelled last night?

   B: Yes, _____.

6. A: Can you take all five of us home?

B: No, _____.

7. A: Why are you yawning?

B: *Because I didn't drink enough coffee* _____.

8. A: Why is the lemonade sour?

B: _____.

9. A: What happened to the garden?

B: _____.

10. A: Why is the crime rate so high here?

B: _____.

11. A: Why aren't the clothes clean?

B: _____.

12. A: Why is one wall yellow?

B: _____.

21 Practice

Gabe and Cindy are going camping. Complete the sentences with *enough* + a noun from the list.

batteries	food	sunscreen
clothes	gas	time
equipment	information	water
film	matches	
flashlights	money	

Gabe: I have two shirts, a sweatshirt,

and two pairs of jeans. Do I have

enough clothes?
                1

Cindy: I think so. I have the camping stove. Do we have _____ to
                                                                    2

light it?

Gabe: I'll get some more. Look in those bottles. Is there _____
3</br>?

Cindy: No, we need to get some more. What about meals? Is there

_____?
4</br>

Gabe: We have a lot of food. Don't worry. Is the car ready? Do we have

_____?
5</br>

Cindy: Yes, but we need more cash. We don't have _____.
6</br>

Gabe: Okay. Do we have _____? I got sunburned last time.
7</br>

Cindy: Yes, we do. It might be dark when we get there. Do we have

_____ and _____?
8   9</br>

Gabe: Yes, they are already in the car. I found my camera. Is there

_____?
10</br>

Cindy: I'm not sure.

Gabe: Okay. Do we have everything else? Sleeping bags, tent? Do we have

_____?
11</br>

Cindy: Yes, I think we've got everything. Do you know where this place is? Do we have

_____?
12</br>

Gabe: Yes, I have a map and good directions, so let's go! We want to get there before

night. Do we have _____?
13</br>

Cindy: We'll leave in 20 minutes. We'll be fine.

SELF-TEST

A   Choose the best answer, A, B, C, or D, to complete the sentence. Mark your answer by darkening the oval with the same letter.

1. _____ the dishes come with a salad.

   A. All of   Ⓐ Ⓑ Ⓒ Ⓓ
   B. Very
   C. Every
   D. Enough

2. The suitcase is _____ heavy. I can't lift it.

   A. all of   Ⓐ Ⓑ Ⓒ Ⓓ
   B. too
   C. every
   D. enough

3. He's _____ tired. He needs to see a doctor.

   A. all of   Ⓐ Ⓑ Ⓒ Ⓓ
   B. very
   C. every
   D. enough

4. _____ lesson is interesting.

   A. All of   Ⓐ Ⓑ Ⓒ Ⓓ
   B. Very
   C. Every
   D. Enough

5. That jacket is too expensive _____ Jamie to buy.

   A. too   Ⓐ Ⓑ Ⓒ Ⓓ
   B. very
   C. for
   D. enough

6. Some of _____ are sleeping.

   A. the child   Ⓐ Ⓑ Ⓒ Ⓓ
   B. the children
   C. children
   D. child

7. Min isn't _____ to drive.

   A. old enough   Ⓐ Ⓑ Ⓒ Ⓓ
   B. old too
   C. enough
   D. enough old

8. They didn't have _____ to finish the test.

   A. time enough   Ⓐ Ⓑ Ⓒ Ⓓ
   B. time too
   C. too many
   D. enough time

9. Almost all of the women _____ at the camera.

   A. is looking   Ⓐ Ⓑ Ⓒ Ⓓ
   B. looks
   C. are looking
   D. was looking

10. The bed was _____ cold for her to sleep in.

    A. too   Ⓐ Ⓑ Ⓒ Ⓓ
    B. very
    C. for
    D. enough

B **Find the underlined word or phrase, A, B, C, or D, that is incorrect. Mark your answer by darkening the oval with the same letter.**

1. <u>All of</u> the <u>men</u> <u>is wearing</u> <u>hats</u>.
   A   B   C   D

   Ⓐ Ⓑ Ⓒ Ⓓ

2. <u>Some of</u> the <u>music</u> <u>are</u> <u>new</u>.
   A   B   C   D

   Ⓐ Ⓑ Ⓒ Ⓓ

3. <u>There were</u> <u>too much</u> <u>sandwiches</u> and not
   A   B   C
   <u>enough drinks</u>.
   D

   Ⓐ Ⓑ Ⓒ Ⓓ

4. <u>The coffee</u> <u>is</u> <u>too weak</u>. It's not
   A   B   C
   <u>enough strong</u>.
   D

   Ⓐ Ⓑ Ⓒ Ⓓ

5. <u>The food was</u> <u>enough greasy</u> <u>for her</u> <u>to eat</u>.
   A   B   C   D

   Ⓐ Ⓑ Ⓒ Ⓓ

6. <u>He has</u> <u>too much</u> <u>problems</u> and not
   A   B   C
   <u>enough money</u>.
   D

   Ⓐ Ⓑ Ⓒ Ⓓ

7. <u>This dinner isn't</u> <u>cheap too</u>. It's
   A   B
   <u>too expensive</u> <u>for us to eat</u> here often.
   C   D

   Ⓐ Ⓑ Ⓒ Ⓓ

8. It's <u>too difficult</u> <u>for me</u> <u>pass</u> the test. I
   A   B   C
   didn't <u>study enough</u>.
   D

   Ⓐ Ⓑ Ⓒ Ⓓ

9. <u>Every men</u> in the room <u>is working</u>
   A   B
   <u>hard enough</u>. They're <u>very</u> tired.
   C   D

   Ⓐ Ⓑ Ⓒ Ⓓ

10. <u>I'm not</u> <u>enough tall</u> <u>to reach</u> the window.
    A   B   C
    I'm <u>too short</u>.
    D

   Ⓐ Ⓑ Ⓒ Ⓓ

UNIT 10
OBJECTS AND PRONOUNS

10a Object Pronouns

Student Book 1 p. 246, Student Book 1B p. 54

1 Practice

Rewrite the sentences. Replace the underlined words in each sentence with an object pronoun.

1. Danny loves <u>his new car</u>.

   Danny loves it .

2. Tara ate <u>the oranges</u>.

   _____ .

3. I don't know <u>his phone number</u>.

   _____ .

4. I'm going on vacation with <u>my son</u>.

   _____ .

5. Jay is talking to <u>his wife</u>.

   _____ .

6. I put <u>the shoes</u> next to the chair.

   _____ .

7. We did <u>the homework</u> in class.

   _____ .

8. They named <u>their daughter</u> Madelyn.

   _____ .

9. Christine is calling <u>her boyfriend</u>.

   _____ .

10. Fernando didn't see <u>the movie</u>.

    _____ .

2 Practice

Rewrite the sentences. Replace the underlined words in each sentence with an object pronoun.

1. Jana is reading <u>the story</u>.

   Jana is reading it .

2. She's reading the story to <u>the children</u>.

   _____ .

3. The children love <u>Jana</u>.

   _____ .

4. Jana's husband, Louis, drives <u>a city bus</u>.

   _____ .

5. Louis drives <u>Jana</u> to work every morning.

   _____ .

6. Louis takes <u>people</u> to work.

   _____ .

7. People enjoy riding <u>the bus</u>.

   _____ .

8. Jana and Louis bought <u>a new house</u> last year.

   _____ .

9. They planted a lot of <u>trees</u> in the yard.

   _____ .

10. We like <u>Jana and Louis</u> very much.

    _____ .

3 Practice

Rewrite the sentences. Replace the underlined words with subject or object pronouns.

1. <u>Fran</u> is my sister.

   She is my sister .

2. She works on <u>a computer</u>.

   _____ .

3. She and I are twins.

_____.

4. Fran, my friend Ann, and I have dance class on Saturday.

_____.

5. The teacher teaches Fran, Ann, and me.

_____.

6. Mrs. Jordan and Mr. Byrd are our teachers.

_____.

7. We like Mrs. Jordan.

_____.

8. Mr. Byrd teaches ballet.

_____.

9. We admire Mr. Byrd.

_____.

10. He is very patient with all the students.

_____.

4 Practice

Rewrite the sentences. Replace the underlined words with subject or object pronouns.

1. Helen works with three women.

  _Helen works with them_____.

2. They ride bicycles to work.

_____.

3. Helen invited my friends and me to her house for dinner.

_____.

4. The dinner is on Friday.

_____.

5. We're going to give Helen some flowers.

_____.

6. She will love <u>the flowers</u>.

_____.

7. Helen is going to make <u>pasta</u>.

_____.

8. <u>Derek</u> is going to make a salad.

_____.

9. We'll help <u>Derek</u>.

_____.

10. When we finish dinner, we'll thank <u>Helen and Derek</u>.

_____.

5 **Practice**

Complete the sentences with the correct pronouns.

A. My brother, Michael, watches too much TV.

_____*It*_____'s on all the time. Most of his
     1

friends watch _____, too.
             2

_____ doesn't get enough exercise.
     3

My parents are worried about _____.
                4

_____ tell Michael to go outside, but
     5

he usually doesn't. Michael isn't doing well in his

classes. He's not going to pass _____. I love my brother. He told
                                  6

_____ he isn't happy, and I'm sad about this.
     7

B. My girlfriend is in Russia. I miss _____ very much. _____ is a
                                1   2

happy person. _____ call her every week, and _____ writes email
                   3   4

to me every day. _____ are going to get married in two years. We'll live
                   5

with my parents for six months, but we don't want to stay with _____ for
                                                              6

a long time.

6 **Practice**

Underline the direct object and circle the indirect object in each sentence.

1. My father gave <u>20 dollars</u> to (us).
2. Ricardo lent the book to DeeDee.
3. My wife sent the letter to our daughter.
4. Mom passed the pasta to me.
5. We told the story to the police.
6. My husband passed the box to me.
7. I showed the present to him.
8. My best friend emailed the joke to me.
9. Who mailed the package to the school?
10. They sent a postcard to us from their vacation.
11. I handed the papers back to the class.
12. Luke told the secret to us.
13. Hannah sent the cookies to the boys.
14. The bank lent the money to my parents.
15. My mother gave the photos to us.
16. I handed the flowers to her.
17. She gave the information to us.
18. I gave the toys to you.

7 **Practice**

Rewrite the sentences from Practice 6 to change the position of the indirect object. The sentences should have the same meaning. Do not use *to*.

1. *My father gave us 20 dollars* .
2. _____ .
3. _____ .
4. _____ .

5. _____ .

6. _____ .

7. _____ .

8. _____ .

9. _____ ?

10. _____ .

11. _____ .

12. _____ .

13. _____ .

14. _____ .

15. _____ .

16. _____ .

17. _____ .

18. _____ .

8 Practice

There is a bad phone connection. Ron has to repeat what he says. Underline the direct objects. Then change the direct objects to pronouns and rewrite the sentences using *to*.

1. Ron: Dad lent Steve <u>the car</u>.

   John: Who did he lend it to?

   Ron: *He lent it to Steve.*

2. Ron: Steve showed his friends the car.

   John: Who did he show it to?

   Ron: _____ .

3. Ron: Steve's friends gave him a present.

John: Who gave it to him?

Ron: _____ .

4. Ron: His girlfriend mailed him a card.

John: Who mailed it to him?

Ron: _____ .

5. Ron: He showed me the card.

John: Who did he show it to?

Ron: _____ .

9 Practice

Underline the direct objects. Then change the direct objects to pronouns and rewrite the sentences using *to*.

1. I wrote my best friend <u>a letter</u>.

   I wrote it to my best friend _____ .

2. She sent me a present.

   _____ .

3. I showed my sister the present. It was a sweater.

   _____ .

4. My sister told me a story.

   _____ .

5. I lent my sister the sweater.

   _____ .

6. My sister gave me back the sweater.

   _____ .

7. She lent me $15.00.

   _____ .

10c Indirect Objects with *For*

Student Book 1 p. 253, Student Book 1B p. 61

10 Practice

Pamela is sick. Complete the sentences about her family with *to* or *for*.

1. Pam's husband is going to fix the door ____*for*____ her.

2. Her husband is going to prepare dinner _____ her.

3. Her son passed the orange juice _____ her.

4. Her daughter is going to open a window _____ her.

5. He's going to give the aspirin _____ her.

6. Her daughter is going to answer the phone _____ her.

11 Practice

You don't feel well. Make requests of your best friend. Use *for* and the prompts.

1. buy/flowers

   Could you buy some flowers for me _____ ?

2. get/homework

   _____ ?

3. open/door

   _____ ?

4. prepare/soup

   _____ ?

5. answer/phone

   _____ ?

6. get/water

   _____ ?

12 Practice

You're planning a party. Write sentences using *to* or *for* and the prompts.

1. email/invitations/friends

   We're going to email invitations to our friends _____ .

2. prepare/food/party

_____.

3. open/door/guests

_____.

4. offer/drinks/friends

_____.

5. show/video of our vacation/guests

_____.

6. play/music/guests

_____.

10d Indirect Objects with Certain Verbs

Student Book 1 p. 255, Student Book 1B p. 63

| 13 | Practice

Mr. and Mrs. Daniels's house caught on fire. Everyone is okay, but they need some things. Their neighbors are helping. Complete the sentences with the words in parentheses.

1. Don bought (some food/them).

_Don bought some food for them_____.

2. I made (some bread/them).

_____.

_____.

3. My mom offered (our living room/them).

_____.

4. My sister got (some clothes/children).

_____.

5. The firefighters explained (the cause of the fire/Mrs. Daniels).

_____.

6. When the fire started, my dad called 911. The operator repeated (the address/him)

_____.

7. They saved the computer, but it doesn't work. My brother's going to fix (it/them).

_____.

|14| Practice

Read the sentences. Circle _to_ or _for_.

1. I got a new radio (to / for) my brother.

2. We made a cake (to / for) our class.

3. They explained the rules (to / for) the children.

4. Rudy got flowers (to / for) his girlfriend.

5. My uncle introduced my mother (to / for) my father.

6. Sheldon bought a new car (to / for) his mother.

7. She repeated the address (to / for) the pizza company.

8. Mr. Miller explained the homework (to / for) us.

9. My son made a birthday card (to / for) me.

10. The police repeated the instructions (to / for) us.

|15| Practice

Tammy and David went out, and their 14-year-old daughter stayed home with her younger brother. Write sentences using _to_ or _for_ and the prompts.

1. Tammy and David/explain/rules/daughter

    Tammy and David explained the rules to their daughter .

2. They/show/emergency numbers/her

_____.

3. They/explain/bedtimes/her

_____.

4. David/make/reservations/them

_____.

5. Tammy/bought/a new watch/David

_____.

6. Tammy and David/repeat/instructions/her one more time

_____.

| 16 | **Practice**

Katie and William had a new baby. Write sentences using _to_ or _for_ and the prompts.

1. William/bought/new suitcase/his wife

_____.

2. He/open/door/her

_____.

3. At the hospital, the doctor show/picture of baby/them

_____.

4. The doctor/explain/procedure/them

_____.

5. The baby came! Katie/introduced/William/their new son

_____.

6. William/bought/new ring/his wife

_____.

7. Katie's sister/got/flowers/her

_____.

Practice

Tanya and Stan moved into a new house. Their next-door neighbor Tim helped them. Write sentences using *to* or *for* and the prompts.

1. Tim/made/dinner/them

   _____.

2. He/show/the town/them

   _____.

3. He/introduce/them/other people

   _____.

4. Tanya and Stan/wrote/thank you card/Tim

   _____.

10e Possessive Pronouns

Student Book 1 p. 258, Student Book 1B p. 66

18 Practice

Circle the possessive pronoun or adjective in parentheses.

1. A: Is that ((my) / mine) laptop?
   B: No, (you / yours) is in the bedroom.
   A: Are these (my / mine) keys?
   B: No, those are (my / mine). (You / Yours) are on the table.
      Don't forget (your / yours) lunch.
   A: That's (my / mine)? Thanks!

2. A: Is that (your / yours) dog?
   B: No, (our / ours) dog is sleeping in the corner.

3. A: Where did I put (my / mine) coffee?
   B: Is this (you / yours)?
   A: Yes, thanks!

4. A: Where should we have the party?
   B: (My / Mine) house is too small. (Your / Yours) isn't big enough either. Let's ask
      Diane. Maybe we can have it at (her / hers).

5. A: Who didn't do (their / theirs) dishes?
   B: I did (my / mine) dishes.
   C: I did (my / mine).
   D: Okay, okay, they're (my / mine).

6. A: Is that Harry and Kelly's house?
   B: No, (their / theirs) is yellow and white.
   A: Is it a big house?
   B: Yes, but (our / ours) is bigger.

7. A: My class is really good.
   B: (Our / Ours) isn't. It's too big. Mrs. Kaufman is (our / ours) teacher. (Her / Hers) tests are too hard. Maybe I'll come to (your / yours) class.

8. A: We have (our / ours) tickets. Do you have (you / yours)?
   B: Not yet.
   C: I did, but I lost (my / mine)!

9. I remember his name, but I forget (her / hers).

10. A: These CDs are (our / ours).
   B: No, they're not. They're (their / theirs).
   A: Well, they look like (our / ours).
   B: A little bit, but (their / theirs) are new.

11. A: Hey, stop. That's (her / hers) ice cream.
   B: No it isn't. (Her / Hers) is over there. This is (my / mine).

12. A: What kind of sandwich do you have?
   B: I have cheese.
   A: I have peanut butter.
   B: Do you want to trade? I'll give you (my / mine) and you give me (your / yours).

19 | Practice

Complete the sentences with *it's* or *its*.

1. ___It's___ a beautiful day today.

2. _____ a little cold but sunny.

3. Our tree is losing _____ leaves.

4. The radio is on. _____ music is playing softly.

5. Our tire swing is gently moving on _____ rope.

6. Our house looks nice in _____ new color.

7. _____ 1:30 right now.

8. _____ my favorite time of year.

20 Practice

Complete the sentences with *it's* or *its*.

1. A: Here's one sock. Where's _____ mate?

   B: _____ on the floor. Hey, _____ time to go.

2. A: _____ not working. What's wrong with this computer?

   B: There's coffee in _____ keys. _____ not a strong computer.

3. A: This cake is delicious!

   B: _____ a family recipe. _____ secret is to put a little coffee in it before you bake it.

10f Indefinite Pronouns

Student Book 1 p. 263, Student Book 1B p. 71

21 Practice

Complete the sentences with *something, someone, anything, anyone, nothing* or *no one*.

1. A: What do you want for your birthday?

   B: I don't want _____*anything*_____. I have enough stuff.

2. A: Is there _____ wrong?

   B: No, _____.

3. I'm hungry. I didn't have _____ to eat all day.

4. We called Jim's house, but _____ answered.

5. Mother: What are you eating?

   Son: _____!

6. A: Shhhh. _____ is coming.

   B: Who is it?

7. A: Turn around. There's _____ on your jacket.

    B: What is it?

    A: A piece of paper.

8. Answering machine: _____ is here to take your call.

                      Please leave a message.

9. A: _____ locked the door and I don't have a key.

    B: Ask at the reception desk.

    A: I didn't see _____ at the desk.

10. A: There was _____ on the train this morning.

    B: That's because it's a holiday.

11. A: I'm bored. I don't have _____ to do.

    B: You're lucky. I have too much to do.

12. A: What's that? I hear _____ in the kitchen.

    B: I'll go see.

    A: Well?

    B: It was _____ . I didn't see _____ .

13. A: I'm hot. I want _____ cold to drink.

    B: There's _____ here. I'll go to the store.

14. I want _____ sweet, but _____ too sweet.

15. Theresa is going to France, but she doesn't know _____ there.

16. Customer: I'll have the soup.

    Waiter: Do you want _____ to drink with that?

    Customer: No, thanks.

17. A: Did you have fun downtown?

    B: Yes, but I didn't find _____ to buy.

    A: _____ ?

18. A: There's _____ good on TV tonight. Do you want to go out?

B: Sure, but I don't have _____ to wear.

A: I'll lend you _____ of mine.

19. A: Look at that star.

B: Where? I don't see _____.

20. A: Hey, I think you've got _____ from your mom.

B: What is it?

A: It looks like a letter.

21. A: There's _____ in the window. I see a face!

B: Relax. There's _____ there.

22. Customer: These are nice. Do you have _____ in red?

Sales clerk: I'll look for you.

23. A: There are a lot of cars here, but I don't see _____ in

the store.

B: Maybe it's closed.

24. First teacher: I had a bad day at school.

Second teacher: What happened?

First teacher: _____ did the homework.

25. Doctor: I have good news for you. There's _____ wrong with you.

Patient: That's great. Thanks!

26. A: Is _____ there?

B: Let's go. There's _____ here.

27. A: Are you ready for dinner?

B: I don't want _____. I don't feel very well.

28. A: What are you doing?

B: _____.

A: Want to come over? We'll think of _____ to do.

B: Okay. I'll be there in an hour.

SELF-TEST

A   **Choose the best answer, A, B, C, or D, to complete the sentence. Mark your answer by darkening the oval with the same letter.**

1. Those are _____ shoes.

   A. mine   Ⓐ Ⓑ Ⓒ Ⓓ
   B. his
   C. theirs
   D. yours

2. Jason is talking to _____.

   A. her   Ⓐ Ⓑ Ⓒ Ⓓ
   B. his
   C. theirs
   D. she

3. My father lent his car _____ my brother.

   A. her   Ⓐ Ⓑ Ⓒ Ⓓ
   B. for
   C. mine
   D. to

4. Kevin bought flowers _____ her.

   A. her   Ⓐ Ⓑ Ⓒ Ⓓ
   B. for
   C. mine
   D. to

5. Is that pencil _____?

   A. my   Ⓐ Ⓑ Ⓒ Ⓓ
   B. your
   C. their
   D. yours

6. I didn't see _____.

   A. nothing   Ⓐ Ⓑ Ⓒ Ⓓ
   B. something
   C. anything
   D. no one

7. Our teacher didn't give _____ the tests.

   A. we   Ⓐ Ⓑ Ⓒ Ⓓ
   B. us
   C. they
   D. my

8. _____ is in the room.

   A. Anyone   Ⓐ Ⓑ Ⓒ Ⓓ
   B. Them
   C. Anything
   D. No one

9. What is another way to write the following sentence?
   "The doctor handed Mr. Murphy the book."

   A. The doctor handed   Ⓐ Ⓑ Ⓒ Ⓓ
   the book for Mr. Murphy.
   B. The doctor handed Mr. Murphy.
   C. The doctor handed Mr. Murphy mine book.
   D. The doctor handed the book to Mr. Murphy.

10. There's _____ in my eye!

    A. anyone   Ⓐ Ⓑ Ⓒ Ⓓ
    B. something
    C. anything
    D. no one

B Find the underlined word or phrase, A, B, C, or D, that is incorrect. Mark your answer by darkening the oval with the same letter.

1. I offered the juice for them.
   A   B   C   D

   Ⓐ Ⓑ Ⓒ Ⓓ

2. Her car is small, but my is big.
   A   B   C   D

   Ⓐ Ⓑ Ⓒ Ⓓ

3. Hey, there's anyone at the door.
          A   B   C

   Will you get it please?
   D

   Ⓐ Ⓑ Ⓒ Ⓓ

4. That's not yours coffee. It's hers.
   A   B   C   D

   Ⓐ Ⓑ Ⓒ Ⓓ

5. Here's the shoe. Where's it's partner?
   A   B   C   D

   Ⓐ Ⓑ Ⓒ Ⓓ

6. I didn't lose something. There's nothing
     A   B   C   D

   here.

   Ⓐ Ⓑ Ⓒ Ⓓ

7. He made dinner to her, and he bought her
      A   B   C   D

   flowers.

   Ⓐ Ⓑ Ⓒ Ⓓ

8. This apartment is mine. It's not your.
                  A   B   C   D

   Ⓐ Ⓑ Ⓒ Ⓓ

9. We told he the news. The car was his.
      A   B   C   D

   Ⓐ Ⓑ Ⓒ Ⓓ

10. When we asked him, he didn't say
          A   B

    something about it.
    C   D

   Ⓐ Ⓑ Ⓒ Ⓓ

UNIT 11
MODALS

11a *Can*

Student Book 1 p. 270, Student Book 1B p. 78

☐1 Practice

Write sentences about yourself with *I can* or *I can't*.

1. play the guitar

   <u>I can play the guitar</u>   .

2. speak Spanish

   _____.

3. make bread

   _____.

4. drive

   _____.

5. walk to school

   _____.

6. use a computer

   _____.

7. ride horses

   _____.

8. ski

   _____.

9. cook

   _____.

10. fly an airplane

    _____.

11. swim

_____.

12. cut hair

_____.

13. take good photographs

_____.

14. do this exercise

_____.

2 | Practice

Write sentences with *can* or *can't*.

1. my friend Yungbo/do math well

   _My friend Yungbo can't do math well_____.

2. my father/tell funny jokes

   _____.

3. Sarah/use a cell phone

   _____.

4. I/walk on my hands

   _____.

5. my grandmother/write stories

   _____.

6. I/watch my favorite movie many times

   _____.

7. Tony/make pizza

   _____.

8. my nephew/tell time

   _____.

9. David/read Japanese

   _____.

10. they/listen to music and read at the same time

_____.

11. Lauren/make a good cup of tea

_____.

12. my cousin Sonny/play soccer

_____.

11b Questions with _Can_

Student Book 1 p. 273, Student Book 1B p. 81

3 ### Practice

Kay is interviewing for a new job. Read the job requirements and then read about Kay. Write questions and answers using the prompts.

Kay	Job Requirements
types	type
uses computers	use computer
speaks Korean	speak Arabic
never learned to drive	drive
loves working with people	work well with people
has two young children	travel a lot
works hard	sometimes work nine hours a day

1. A. Interviewer: _Can you type_ ?

B. Kay: _Yes, I can_ .

2. A. Interviewer: _____?

B. Kay: _____.

3. A. Interviewer: _____?

B. Kay: _____.

4. A. Interviewer: _____?

B. Kay: _____.

5. A. Interviewer: _____?

B. Kay: _____.

6. A. Interviewer: _____ ?

   B. Kay: _____ .

7. A. Interviewer: _____ ?

   B. Kay: _____ .

4 | Practice

Complete the sentences using *can* or *can't* and phrases from the list or your own.

cook	play sports
drive well	sing
explain English grammar	swim
play games	work well with people

1. My father *can sing very well* _____ .

2. My mother _____ .

3. _____ my best friend _____ ?

4. My brothers and sisters _____ .

5. _____ my teachers _____ ?

6. _____ my classmates _____ ?

5 | Practice

Write questions and answers about what the following people can and can't do.

1. teachers

   Can teachers write well _____ ?

   Yes, they can _____ .

2. doctors

   _____ ?

   _____ .

3. cooks

   _____ ?

   _____ .

4. teenagers

_____?

_____.

5. babies

_____?

_____.

6. college students

_____?

_____.

7. the police

_____?

_____.

8. musicians

_____?

_____.

9. artists

_____?

_____.

10. your friends

_____?

_____.

11. your boss

_____?

_____.

12. your neighbors

_____?

_____.

11c *Could:* Past of *Can*

Student Book 1 p. 275, Student Book 1B p. 83

6 Practice

Jack is 30 years old. Write sentences about what he can do now that he couldn't do when he was two years old. Use phrases from the list.

pay bills	talk
reach tall shelves	tell time
read	tie his shoes
shave	use a computer
stay up late	walk well

1. *He couldn't pay bills then,*
   but he can now .

2. _____ .

3. _____ .

4. _____ .

5. _____ .

6. _____ .

7. _____ .

8. _____ .

9. _____ .

10. _____ .

7 Practice

Stephanie is 23 years old. Write sentences about what she can do now that she couldn't do when she was five years old. Use phrases from the list.

cook pasta	go to bed at midnight
cross the street alone	take the bus
do laundry	travel
drink wine	use a bankcard
eat spicy food	vote

1. *She couldn't cook pasta then, but she can now* .

60

Unit 11

2. _____ .

3. _____ .

4. _____ .

5. _____ .

6. _____ .

7. _____ .

8. _____ .

9. _____ .

10. _____ .

8 Practice

There was a big snowstorm and the Williams family was inside their house for five hours. The electricity was off. Write sentences about what they could and couldn't do. Use phrases from the list.

cook anything   play cards
go online   read a newspaper
go outside   tell stories
light candles   use the microwave
make a sandwich   watch any DVDs

1. *They couldn't cook anything* _____ .

2. _____ .

3. _____ .

4. _____ .

5. _____ .

6. _____ .

7. _____ .

8. _____ .

9. _____ .

10. _____ .

9 Practice

Judy was on a 14-hour flight to Australia. Write sentences about what she could and couldn't do. Use phrases from the list.

meet people	ride her bicycle	sleep	take a shower
read	run	smoke	watch movies

1. _She could meet people_ .
2. _____ .
3. _____ .
4. _____ .
5. _____ .
6. _____ .
7. _____ .
8. _____ .

11d Be Able To

Student Book 1 p. 278, Student Book 1B p. 86

10 Practice

Read about Denise's experience one night. Change the underlined forms of *can* and *could* to forms of *be able to*.

I was walking one night when I fell into a big hole.

I <u>couldn't see</u> the opening, and I <u>couldn't hear</u> anyone.
   1   2

I was afraid. I <u>couldn't feel</u> one of my feet, but I <u>could find</u>
           3   4

the matches in my pocket. I lit the matches, and I felt better.

I started to call "Help!" No one <u>could hear</u> me. I finally slept.
                        5

   When I woke up, I <u>could see</u> the sky, and I <u>could hear</u>
              6   7

traffic. I called out for help again. Finally, a young man looked down the hole, and he

<u>could see</u> me! He said he <u>could borrow</u> a cell phone to call 911. The firefighters came and
 8   9

<u>could get</u> me out of the hole. I was okay.
 10

   I still have bad dreams sometimes, and I <u>can't sleep</u> without a light on, but now
                                  11

I <u>can talk</u> about my story.
 12

1. _wasn't able to see_ _____

2. _____

3. _____

4. _____

5. _____

6. _____

7. _____

8. _____

9. _____

10. _____

11. _____

12. _____

II Practice

Read about Craig's fishing experience. Change the underlined forms of *can* and *could* to forms of *be able to*.

I don't like fishing because I <u>can't swim</u>. One Saturday, my friends invited me to go
₁
with them. I got a fishing license because you <u>can't fish</u> without it. I was in the boat, and
₂
I <u>couldn't stay</u> awake because the sun was so hot. Suddenly, I <u>could feel</u> something pull
₃ ₄
on my line. I looked in the water, and I <u>could see</u> this big, big fish. He was really heavy! I
₅
<u>couldn't bring</u> him into the boat. My friends were giving me advice, but I <u>couldn't hear</u>
₆ ₇
them. I was busy. The fish broke the line and swam away, but now I <u>can tell</u> people about
₈
the big fish I almost caught.

1. _am not able to swim_ _____   5. _____

2. _____   6. _____

3. _____   7. _____

4. _____   8. _____

Practice

Rachel is 13 years old. Write sentences to say what she can do now, what she could do when she was a year old, and what she will be able to do when she's 21.

One year	Now (age 13)	Age 21
laugh	go to junior high school	vote
sit up	take care of her brothers	ski
crawl	play the guitar	go to college
drink milk	go out with her friends	get an apartment

1. When she was a year old, <u>*she could laugh*</u> (OR) <u>*she was able to laugh*</u>.

2. Now, _____.

3. At age 21, _____.

4. When she was a year old, _____.

5. Now, _____.

6. At age 21, _____.

7. When she was a year old, _____.

8. Now, _____.

9. At age 21, _____.

10. When she was a year old, _____.

11. Now, _____.

12. At age 21, _____.

13 | Practice

Tim is 32 years old. Write sentences to say what he can do now, what he could do when he was five years old, and what he will be able to do when he's 65.

Five years	Now (age 32)	Age 65
take naps every day	have children	stop working
say the alphabet	get married	play with his grandchildren
read his name	buy a house	play golf
start school	learn English at night	travel

1. When he was five years old, _____ *he could take naps every day* _____

   (OR) *he was able to take naps every day* _____.

2. Now, _____

   _____.

3. At age 65, _____

   _____.

4. When he was five years old, _____

   _____.

5. Now, _____

   _____.

6. At age 65, _____

   _____.

7. When he was five years old, _____

   _____.

8. Now, _____

   _____.

9. At age 65, _____

   _____.

10. When he was five years old, _____

   _____.

11. Now, _____

_____ .

12. At age 65, _____

_____ .

11e *Should*

Student Book 1 p. 281, Student Book 1B p. 89

14 Practice

Richard is moving into his first apartment. Complete the sentences with *should* or *shouldn't*.

1. He _____ pay rent on time.

2. He _____ be noisy.

3. He _____ have big parties.

4. He _____ meet the other people in the building.

5. He _____ talk to his roommate about money before they move in together.

6. They _____ decide how to divide the housework.

15 Practice

Beverly wants to lose weight. Complete the sentences with *should* or *shouldn't*.

1. She _____ talk to a doctor first.

2. She _____ exercise.

3. She _____ eat late at night.

4. She _____ drink a lot of alcohol.

5. She _____ healthy food.

6. She _____ eat breakfast.

16 **Practice**

Laura is a lonely student. Write sentences with *should* or *shouldn't*.

1. She doesn't smile.

   _She should smile_____.

2. She stays home.

   _____.

3. She doesn't call her classmates.

   _____.

4. She is unfriendly.

   _____.

5. She doesn't listen to others.

   _____.

6. She doesn't invite people to her house.

   _____.

7. She doesn't look at people.

   _____.

8. She doesn't ask people about their interests.

   _____.

17 **Practice**

Read the situations. Write sentences about what you should or shouldn't do.

1. You feel sick.

   _I should see a doctor,_____ (OR) _I should take some aspirin,_

2. You're late for class.

   _____.

3. You don't understand the teacher.

   _____.

4. You feel sleepy.

   _____.

5. You cut your finger.

_____.

6. You don't like your roommate.

_____.

7. You are homesick.

_____.

8. You go to a dinner party in the United States.

_____.

9. You forget your homework.

_____.

10. You're driving, and you see the police.

_____.

11. You walk home late at night.

_____.

12. You don't have enough money.

_____.

11f Must

Student Book 1 p. 284, Student Book 1B p. 92

18 Practice

Read the following dorm rules. Complete the sentences with _must_ or _mustn't_.

1. You _____must_____ turn off your music at 9:00 P.M.

2. You _____ paint the room.

3. You _____ smoke in the room.

4. You _____ cook in the room.

5. You _____ be quiet after 11:00 P.M.

6. You _____ have guests overnight.

7. You _____ have big parties.

8. You _____ clean your bathroom.

9. You _____ have pets.

10. You _____ sign visitors in at the front desk.

19 Practice

Read the following driving rules. Complete the sentences with *must* or *mustn't*.

1. You _____ study for the test.

2. You _____ practice driving before you take the test.

3. You _____ stop at red lights.

4. You _____ drive too fast.

5. You _____ wear your seatbelt.

6. You _____ drink and drive.

7. You _____ drive if you are sleepy.

8. You _____ pay attention all the time.

9. You _____ talk on your cell phone.

10. You _____ look in your mirrors for other cars.

20 Practice

Fred broke his leg last week. Read his doctor's rules. Complete the sentences with *must* or *mustn't*.

1. He _____ stay off his foot.

2. He _____ keep his foot up.

3. He _____ walk.

4. He _____ put ice on it.

5. He _____ take aspirin every six hours.

6. He _____ stand up for long periods of time.

21 Practice

Read about how to take a photograph. Complete the sentences with *must* or *mustn't*.

1. You _____ look through the lens.

2. You _____ stand one meter away.

3. You _____ put fingers in front of the camera.

4. You _____ check the light.

5. You _____ push the button here.

6. You _____ open the camera before you finish the film.

22 Practice

Write what you must or mustn't do in the following situations.

1. before you buy a computer

   _You must look at prices_____.

2. before you live with a roommate

   _____.

3. before you get married

   _____.

4. before you move

   _____.

5. before you have children

   _____.

6. before you have a party

   _____.

7. before you buy a house

   _____.

8. before you go to a job interview

   _____.

9. before you run a marathon

   _____.

10. before you register for classes

_____ .

◈ 11g *Have To*
Student Book 1 p. 288, Student Book 1B p. 96

23 Practice

What do you have to do in your house? Complete the sentences with *have to* or *don't have to*.

1. I _____ clean my room.

2. I _____ make my bed.

3. I _____ do the dishes.

4. I _____ do laundry.

5. I _____ go grocery shopping.

6. I _____ pay rent.

7. I _____ make dinner.

8. I _____ work in the garden.

9. I _____ fix the car.

10. I _____ tell my parents where I'm going and when I'll be back.

24 Practice

Mark works in the stock market. Complete the sentences with *has to* or *doesn't have to*.

1. He _____ be there on time.

2. He _____ work on Saturday.

3. He _____ wear a tie.

4. He _____ work at the office all the time.

5. He _____ be friendly at work.

6. He _____ speak other languages.

7. He _____ work eight hours a day.

8. He _____ travel.

Complete the sentences with *have to/has to* or *don't have to/doesn't have to*.

1. I _____ do my homework now. I can do it later.

2. I _____ go now. I'm going to be late!

3. They _____ to drive. It's too far to walk.

4. We _____ drive. We can walk there.

5. She _____ pick out CDs for the party. She's the DJ.

6. You _____ bring anything. We have everything here.

7. Bessie _____ get good grades. She wants to go to a good college.

8. The class _____ turn in the assignment tomorrow. It is due next week.

9. Jimmy _____ clean his room. It is a mess!

10. Alejandro _____ go the store. He doesn't have anything to eat at home.

11. Akiko _____ study very hard. She is very intelligent, and she remembers everything.

12. David and I _____ go to work now, but we don't want to.

13. You _____ wash it in cold water. Never wash it in hot water.

14. We _____ work tomorrow. It's a holiday!

15. I _____ get new shoes. These are too small.

16. Brenda _____ wear glasses. She can see well.

17. My mother _____ water the garden. The flowers are very dry.

18. I _____ drink something. I'm really thirsty.

19. When _____ you _____ be home?

20. You _____ come to my house. I'll come to yours.

26 Practice
Write questions and short answers using *have to* and information from the chart.

Qualities	Waiter	Musician	Engineer
Have a degree			X
Play the piano and sing		X	
Be friendly	X		

1. waiter/have a degree

   _Does a waiter have to have a degree_____?

   _No she/he doesn't_____.

2. waiter/play the piano and sing

   _____?

   _____.

3. waiter/be friendly

   _____?

   _____.

4. musician/have a degree

   _____?

   _____.

5. musician/play the piano and sing

   _____?

   _____.

6. musician/be friendly

   _____?

   _____.

7. engineer/have a degree

   _____?

   _____.

8. engineer/play the piano and sing

_____ ?

_____ .

9. engineer/be friendly

_____ ?

_____ .

27 Practice

Write about people in different professions. Use _have to/has to_ **or** _don't have to/ doesn't have to_ **and phrases from the list.**

be creative	prevent crime
fly airplanes	think of interesting stories
help people understand ideas	treat sick people

1. teacher

   A teacher has to help people understand ideas .

   A teacher doesn't have to fly airplanes .

2. police officers

   _____ .

   _____ .

3. pilot

   _____ .

   _____ .

4. doctors

   _____ .

   _____ .

5. artist

   _____ .

   _____ .

6. writers

   _____ .

   _____ .

28 Practice

My grandmother often tells us about when she was young. Complete the sentences with *had to* or *didn't have to*.

1. I _____*had to*_____ walk to school.

2. My mother _____ work. She stayed at home.

3. I _____ wear dresses every day.

4. I _____ help take care of my sisters.

5. We _____ lock our doors. We felt very safe with our neighbors.

6. My sisters and I _____ be quiet when guests came over. We couldn't be noisy.

7. We _____ buy vegetables because we had a big garden.

29 Practice

When Hilary was 14 years old, she took care of other people's children. Complete the sentences with *had to* or *didn't have to*.

1. I _____*had to*_____ read the children a story before they went to bed.

2. I _____ stay awake. I could sleep if I felt tired.

3. I _____ arrive on time.

4. I _____ make dinner. The children ate before I got there.

5. I _____ walk home. The parents gave me a ride.

6. I _____ put the children to bed.

7. I _____ know the phone number of where the parents were.

30 Practice

Write questions and answers using *have to* and the prompts.

1. David/work/today

   _Did David have to work today_____ ?

   Yes, _he did_____ .

2. Lynn/do/homework/yesterday

   _____ ?

   No, _____ .

3. Susan and Lisa/go shopping/last night

   _____ ?

   Yes, _____ .

4. the baby/go to bed/early/Saturday

   _____ ?

   Yes, _____ .

5. Roberto/drive to work/yesterday morning

   _____ ?

   No, _____ .

6. Elena/cook dinner/last night

   _____ ?

   Yes, _____ .

31 Practice

Complete the sentences with things you had to or didn't have to do. Use phrases from the list or add your own.

carry an umbrella	see a doctor	turn off the TV
cook dinner	solve a problem	wear sunscreen
go to school	study for a test	work late
go to the library	take the bus	

1. Last night, _I had to work late._ (OR) _I didn't have to take the bus._

2. Yesterday, _____ .

3. _____ on Saturday.

4. _____ on my last vacation.

5. Last week, _____ .

6. _____ last year.

7. _____ two days ago.

8. This morning, _____ .

11h *May I, Can I, and Could I*

Student Book 1 p. 294, Student Book 1B p. 102

32 Practice

Complete the dialogues with *may I, can I,* or *could I* and *you can* or *you can't*.

1. Friend A: _Can I_ _____ borrow $10.00?

    Friend B: Sure.

2. Young sister: _____ go with you?

    Older sister: No, _____ .

3. Friend A: _____ use your computer?

    Friend B: Yes, _____ .

4. Son: _____ borrow the car?

    Father: No, _____ .

5. Daughter: _____ do the dishes later?

    Mother: No, _____ .

6. Customer: _____ smoke here?

    Waiter: Sorry. There is no smoking in the restaurant.

7. Sales clerk: _____ help you?

    Customer: No, thanks.

8. Boss: _____ speak to you?

    Sales clerk: Certainly.

9. **Son:** _____ stay at Robert's house tonight?

   Mother: Yes, _____.

10. **Customer:** _____ speak with the manager?

    Waiter: I'm sorry. She's not here right now.

11. **Customer:** _____ have some more coffee?

    Waiter: Of course.

12. **Son:** _____ watch TV now?

    Father: Did you finish your homework this afternoon?

33 Practice

Write questions and answers with *may I, can I,* or *could I*.

1. You don't understand the homework. You want to ask the teacher a question.

   Q: _May I ask you a question_____?

   A: _Yes, you may_____.

2. You are ordering ice cream. You want vanilla and strawberry.

   Q: _____?

   A: _____.

3. You want to park your car on a busy street. Ask the police officer if you can park here.

   Q: _____?

   A: _____.

4. You want to get a cell phone. Ask your mother.

   Q: _____?

   A: _____.

5. You're going out, and you want to borrow your sister's clothes.

   Q: _____?

   A: _____.

6. You want to change the TV channel. Your brother is also watching TV.

   Q: _____?

   A: _____.

7. You want to use your friend's camera on vacation. Ask to borrow it.

Q: _____ ?

A: _____ .

8. You're taking a test, but your pencil is broken. Ask to borrow one from a friend.

Q: _____ ?

A: _____ .

9. You're eating lunch at a nice restaurant. Ask for a table near the window.

Q: _____ ?

A: _____ .

10. You're on a bus. You're cold. Ask a stranger if it is OK for you to close the window.

Q: _____ ?

A: _____ .

11. You don't have enough time to finish the test. Ask for more time.

Q: _____ ?

A: _____ .

12. You want a dog. Ask your roommate.

Q: _____ ?

A: _____ .

13. You're on the bus. Someone puts down a newspaper. Ask to read it.

Q: _____ ?

A: _____ .

14. You want to borrow a car. Ask a friend.

Q: _____ ?

A: _____ .

A **Choose the best answer, A, B, C, or D, to complete the sentence. Mark your answer by darkening the oval with the same letter.**

1. I _____ write with my left and my right hand when I was young, but now I can't.

    A. could Ⓐ Ⓑ Ⓒ Ⓓ
    B. should
    C. have to
    D. must

2. They _____ meet us tomorrow. They don't have other plans.

    A. could Ⓐ Ⓑ Ⓒ Ⓓ
    B. didn't have to
    C. had to
    D. can

3. Rose is still working, and it's 12:00. She _____ go to bed.

    A. should Ⓐ Ⓑ Ⓒ Ⓓ
    B. didn't have to
    C. had to
    D. was able to

4. _____ help you?

    A. Couldn't Ⓐ Ⓑ Ⓒ Ⓓ
    B. Didn't have to
    C. May I
    D. Must

5. When you were a child, what _____ you do?

    A. could Ⓐ Ⓑ Ⓒ Ⓓ
    B. didn't have to
    C. had to
    D. can

6. We _____ eat or drink in the library.

    A. could I Ⓐ Ⓑ Ⓒ Ⓓ
    B. mustn't
    C. am able to
    D. can I

7. Steven _____ wear a suit to work. He has to wear a tie, too.

    A. must Ⓐ Ⓑ Ⓒ Ⓓ
    B. could
    C. had to
    D. can

8. _____ borrow your bicycle?

    A. Can Ⓐ Ⓑ Ⓒ Ⓓ
    B. May
    C. Should
    D. Could I

9. She _____ work. Her family has a lot of money.

    A. could Ⓐ Ⓑ Ⓒ Ⓓ
    B. doesn't have to
    C. can
    D. must

10. You _____ stay in bed. You don't feel well.

    A. should Ⓐ Ⓑ Ⓒ Ⓓ
    B. didn't have to
    C. could
    D. will be able to

B Find the underlined word or phrase, A, B, C, or D, that is incorrect. Mark your answer by darkening the oval with the same letter.

1. James <u>must to go now</u>, <u>but</u> he <u>can come</u>
A   B   C   D
   back tomorrow.

   Ⓐ Ⓑ Ⓒ Ⓓ

2. We <u>have to</u> <u>take a test</u> tomorrow. <u>But we</u>
A   B   C
   <u>won't be able to</u> study yesterday.
   D

   Ⓐ Ⓑ Ⓒ Ⓓ

3. Debbie <u>can't ride</u> <u>a bicycle</u> <u>when she</u> was
A   B   C
   <u>ten years old</u>.
   D

   Ⓐ Ⓑ Ⓒ Ⓓ

4. <u>A whale</u> <u>can swim</u>, but <u>it can't</u> <u>to fly</u>.
A   B   C   D

   Ⓐ Ⓑ Ⓒ Ⓓ

5. You <u>must</u> <u>should have</u> a passport before
A   B
   <u>you can</u> <u>travel</u>.
   C   D

   Ⓐ Ⓑ Ⓒ Ⓓ

6. Bill <u>must to</u> <u>get up</u> at 5:30. He <u>has to</u> <u>be</u>
A   B   C   D
   at work at 7:00.

   Ⓐ Ⓑ Ⓒ Ⓓ

7. They <u>have to</u> <u>go to work</u>. <u>They</u> can stay
A   B   C   D
   home.

   Ⓐ Ⓑ Ⓒ Ⓓ

8. She <u>should to study</u>. She <u>has to</u> <u>take</u> a
A   B   C   D
   test tomorrow.

   Ⓐ Ⓑ Ⓒ Ⓓ

9. They <u>are able to</u> <u>help</u> you. <u>What do you</u>
A   B   C
   <u>must to</u> do?
   D

   Ⓐ Ⓑ Ⓒ Ⓓ

10. You <u>aren't able to</u> <u>come</u> with us now, but
A   B
   <u>can</u> you <u>to meet</u> us next week?
   C   D

   Ⓐ Ⓑ Ⓒ Ⓓ

UNIT 12
SPECIAL EXPRESSIONS

12a *Let's*

Student Book 1 p. 300, Student Book 1B p. 108

1 | Practice

Write a response to each statement using *let's* and an expression from the list.

build a fire	have a beach party	play games
cook some corn	invite Jesse and Eric	sing some songs

1. What do you want to do tonight? *Let's have a beach party* .

2. Good idea! Who should we invite?

_____ .

3. What should we do if it gets cold?

_____ .

4. I'm going to be hungry.

_____ .

5. I think Jesse has a guitar.

_____ .

6. The children will be there.

_____ .

2 Practice

It's Raphael's first day at school. He's talking to his new roommate Pierre. Write a response to each statement using *let's* and an expression from the list.

meet our neighbors   talk to an advisor
move the furniture   walk around campus
put some interesting pictures on the walls

1. This room is boring.

   _____.

2. The beds are blocking the window.

   _____.

3. I don't know what classes I'm going to take.

   _____.

4. Who lives next to us?

   _____.

5. Where's the cafeteria?

   _____.

3 Practice

Some friends are at a wildlife rescue farm. Write a response to each statement using *let's* and an expression from the list.

get something to eat
go home now
go see the mountain lions
look at the peacock
read about them
watch the film

1. Here's some information about kangaroos.

   _____.

2. I'm hungry.

   _____.

3. I want to see the big animals.

_____.

4. Sam wants to see the peacock.

_____.

5. Here is a short film about wildlife rescue.

_____.

6. I'm tired. Are you ready to leave?

_____.

4 Practice

Write responses to the statements using *let's* or *let's not*.

1. Here comes the train now!

Let's run _____.

2. The coffee shop is open.

_____.

3. Tomorrow is Vivian's birthday.

_____.

4. The TV isn't working.

_____.

5. I just got a new CD.

_____.

6. That new action movie starts at 9:00.

_____.

7. I have a headache.

_____.

8. Our apartment is too small.

_____.

9. I'm bored.

_____.

10. That street looks dangerous.

_____.

11. Those oranges are cheap!

_____.

12. Uh oh. We are very late!

_____.

12b *Would Like*

Student Book 1 p. 302, Student Book 1B p. 110

5 Practice

Complete the dialogues with *would like*.

1. John: _____*Would*_____ you _____*like*_____ to have dinner with me tonight?

Julia: Sure.

2. John: I _____ a table near the window.

Waiter: Certainly.

3. Waiter: _____ you _____ something to drink?

John: Yes, please.

4. Waiter: _____ you _____ soup or salad?

Julia: I _____ salad, please.

5. Waiter: _____ you _____ rice or a potato?

Julia: Rice.

6. Waiter: _____ you _____ anything else tonight?

John: No, thank you. I _____ the check.

7. John: _____ you _____ to go out with me again sometime?

Julia: Yes. I _____ that.

6 Practice

Write sentences with *would like* or *wouldn't like*.

1. (yes) Susan/go bowling/Saturday

   <u>Susan would like to go bowling on Saturday</u>.

2. (no) Tom/swim/in the ocean

   <u>Tom wouldn't like to swim in the ocean</u>.

3. (yes) Sidney/run/in the New York City Marathon

   _____.

4. (no) He/take/the test early

   _____.

5. (yes) They/feed/the cat

   _____.

6. (no) She/videotape/the party

   _____.

7. (yes) Georgie/plant/tomatoes in the garden

   _____.

8. (no) Pat and Erin/eat/spaghetti tonight

   _____.

12c *Could You* and *Would You*

Student Book 1 p. 306, Student Book 1B p. 114

7 Practice

Benny is going on vacation. He asks his roommate to do things while he's gone. Write his requests using *could you* or *would you* and the prompts.

1. water my plants

   <u>Could you please water my plants</u> ?

2. check my mail

   _____?

3. feed my cat

_____?

4. take me to the airport

_____?

5. write down my phone messages

_____?

6. give the landlord our rent check

_____?

7. pick me up from the airport next week

_____?

---

8 | ## Practice

The Lee family is having a dinner party. Christine asks her husband, Joe, and her two children, Will and Lisa, to do things to prepare. Write her requests using *could you* or *would you* and the prompts.

1. set the table

Lisa, would you please

set the table ?

2. clean your bedrooms

_____?

3. change your clothes

_____?

4. turn off the TV

_____?

5. put on some music

_____?

6. light the candles

_____?

7. wash the lettuce

_____?

9 │ Practice

Write polite questions and answers using the prompts.

1. hold my bag for a minute

A: _Would you hold my bag for a minute_ _____?

B: _Sure. No problem_ _____.

2. close the door

A: _____?

B: _____.

3. tell me where the bank is

A: _____?

B: _____.

4. turn the music down

A: _____?

B: _____.

5. take my letter to the post office

A: _____?

B: _____.

6. smoke outside please

A: _____?

B: _____.

7. drive for a while

A: _____?

B: _____.

12d The Imperative

Student Book 1 p. 308, Student Book 1B p. 116

10 Practice

Put these instructions in the correct order.

How to Send Email

_____ Read the message before you send it.

_____ Click on the "Send" button.

_____ Write your message.

_____ Put your friend's email address in the "To" space.

11 Practice

Put these instructions in the correct order.

How to Make Spaghetti

_____ Put some salt in the water.

_____ Take the pasta out of the water.

_____ Cook for eight to ten minutes.

_____ Put water in a pot.

_____ Boil the water.

_____ Add tomatoes, garlic, and cheese.

_____ Put the spaghetti in the boiling water.

12 Practice

Complete the sentences with affirmative or negative imperatives telling what people should and shouldn't do in the library.

be	keep	put	talk	smoke
eat	make	return	throw away	use

1. _____ cigarettes.

2. _____ quiet.

3. _____ food.

4. _____ loudly.

5. _____ cell phones.

6. _____ reservations to use the computers.

7. _____ books back on the shelf.

8. _____ library clean.

9. _____ your bottles and cans.

10. _____ books in three weeks.

13 Practice

It's Jay's first day at his new job as a waiter. Complete the sentences with affirmative or negative imperatives telling him what to do and what not to do.

be	talk
close	wash
stand	wear
take	

1. _____ polite.

2. _____ your hands.

3. _____ the customers' orders.

4. _____ around with nothing to do.

5. _____ clean uniform.

6. _____ too much to customers.

7. _____ the door when you leave.

A   **Choose the best answer, A, B, C, or D, to complete the sentence. Mark your answer by darkening the oval with the same letter.**

1. _____ go down town tomorrow.

   A. Could   Ⓐ Ⓑ Ⓒ Ⓓ
   B. Let's
   C. Let
   D. Would

2. _____ talk. The students are working.

   A. Could   Ⓐ Ⓑ Ⓒ Ⓓ
   B. Would like
   C. Don't
   D. Would

3. I _____ to have more homework tonight.

   A. wouldn't like   Ⓐ Ⓑ Ⓒ Ⓓ
   B. let's
   C. could
   D. would

4. What country would _____ to live in?

   A. like   Ⓐ Ⓑ Ⓒ Ⓓ
   B. you like
   C. let's
   D. would

5. _____ your books to page 63.

   A. Could you   Ⓐ Ⓑ Ⓒ Ⓓ
   B. Let's
   C. Would you
   D. Open

6. _____ give me some more time?

   A. Could you to   Ⓐ Ⓑ Ⓒ Ⓓ
   B. Would you like
   C. Let
   D. Would you

7. Would they like to come to the beach with us? _____

   A. Yes, they do.   Ⓐ Ⓑ Ⓒ Ⓓ
   B. Yes, let's.
   C. No, they wouldn't.
   D. Yes, they wouldn't.

8. _____ leave at about 9:00.

   A. Would you like   Ⓐ Ⓑ Ⓒ Ⓓ
   B. He
   C. Let's
   D. I would like

9. _____ do the dishes right now. We have to go.

   A. Couldn't   Ⓐ Ⓑ Ⓒ Ⓓ
   B. Don't
   C. Let not
   D. Wouldn't

10. Could you please _____ my car?

   A. to wash   Ⓐ Ⓑ Ⓒ Ⓓ
   B. washed
   C. wash
   D. washing

B **Find the underlined word or phrase, A, B, C, or D, that is incorrect. Mark your answer by darkening the oval with the same letter.**

1. <u>Would</u> you <u>to come</u> with us, or <u>are you</u>
   A   B   C
   <u>too</u> busy?
   D

   Ⓐ Ⓑ Ⓒ Ⓓ

2. <u>Let</u> <u>pick up</u> Jane <u>before</u> <u>we go</u> the party.
   A   B   C   D

   Ⓐ Ⓑ Ⓒ Ⓓ

3. <u>Don't</u> <u>to be</u> late. We <u>have to</u> be there
   A   B   C
   <u>in half an hour</u>.
   D

   Ⓐ Ⓑ Ⓒ Ⓓ

4. <u>Let's</u> <u>don't</u> play the movie right now.
   A   B
   We <u>can do</u> it <u>after dinner</u>.
       C   D

   Ⓐ Ⓑ Ⓒ Ⓓ

5. <u>Could you</u> please <u>to close</u> the window?
   A   B
   <u>I'm</u> really <u>cold</u>.
   C   D

   Ⓐ Ⓑ Ⓒ Ⓓ

6. <u>The light</u> <u>is red</u>. <u>Don't</u> <u>to cross</u> the street.
   A   B   C   D

   Ⓐ Ⓑ Ⓒ Ⓓ

7. Our teacher <u>is giving</u> <u>us</u> a test tomorrow.
                A   B
   <u>Let</u> <u>study</u>.
   C   D

   Ⓐ Ⓑ Ⓒ Ⓓ

8. David <u>would like</u> go with you <u>if</u> <u>you have</u>
          A   B   C
   <u>enough</u> room.
   D

   Ⓐ Ⓑ Ⓒ Ⓓ

9. Frank <u>would to</u> <u>travel</u> <u>to New York</u>
          A   B   C
   <u>for business</u>.
   D

   Ⓐ Ⓑ Ⓒ Ⓓ

10. <u>To sit</u> down and <u>be</u> quiet. <u>People</u>
    A   B   C
    <u>are working</u>.
    D

    Ⓐ Ⓑ Ⓒ Ⓓ

UNIT 13
ADJECTIVES AND ADVERBS

13a Adjectives and Nouns Used as Adjectives

Student Book 1 p. 316, Student Book 1B p. 124

1 Practice

Identify the underlined words. Put an X beside *Noun* or *Adjective*.

1. Christina is a busy <u>mom</u>.   Noun <u>X</u> Adjective ____

2. She has two <u>young</u> children.   Noun ____ Adjective ____

3. They are <u>girls</u>.   Noun ____ Adjective ____

4. Jasmine has <u>blue</u> eyes.   Noun ____ Adjective ____

5. Chloe has <u>brown</u> eyes.   Noun ____ Adjective ____

6. Christina has a full time <u>job</u>.   Noun ____ Adjective ____

7. Her job is <u>interesting</u>.   Noun ____ Adjective ____

8. She is a <u>writer</u>.   Noun ____ Adjective ____

9. She writes books on <u>history</u>.   Noun ____ Adjective ____

10. Sometimes, she writes <u>love</u> stories.   Noun ____ Adjective ____

11. Christina is very <u>happy</u>.   Noun ____ Adjective ____

2 Practice

Identify the underlined words. Put an X beside *Noun* or *Adjective*.

1. Derek is a <u>popular</u> teacher.   Noun ____ Adjective ____

2. He enjoys his <u>students</u>.   Noun ____ Adjective ____

3. Some students are a little <u>lazy</u>.   Noun ____ Adjective ____

4. Some students don't like <u>English</u>.   Noun ____ Adjective ____

5. But Derek likes to work with those <u>students</u>.   Noun ____ Adjective ____

6. Derek is <u>married</u>.   Noun ____ Adjective ____

7. He has a beautiful baby <u>girl</u>.   Noun ____ Adjective ____

8. He and his wife bought a <u>new</u> house.   Noun ____ Adjective ____

9. The house is <u>gray</u> and <u>white</u>.   Noun _____   Adjective _____

10. Derek has a good <u>life</u>.   Noun _____   Adjective _____

3 | Practice

Underline the nouns used as adjectives. There are 12 nouns used as adjectives.

Amanda is a <u>high school</u> student. She is waiting for the school bus near her house. She has a Spanish dictionary, a pencil case, and her gym shoes in her backpack. She doesn't want to be late for her English class. Today she has a history test and then after school, she is going to go to the drama club. On her lunch hour, she buys a sandwich and sits with her friends. There are juice cartons all over the table. The jazz band is playing for the students during lunch. She's going to get a job during her summer vacation.

4 | Practice

Underline the nouns used as adjectives. There are 10 nouns used as adjectives.

Ed wanted to ride his bike downtown, but someone stole his bicycle seat! He had to walk. He met his girlfriend for lunch after her yoga class. When he crossed the street to the restaurant, he didn't see the street light and a car almost hit him! When he got to the sandwich shop, he ordered some fruit salad and a chocolate cookie.

After lunch, Ed and Marcia walked down the street looking in the store windows. They walked around the art museum for an hour, and then they went to Marcia's house. She has a big flower garden. They went into the garden. Marcia took a nap, and Ed read the afternoon newspaper.

5 | Practice

Look at the picture. Complete the names of the objects with words from the list.

| breakfast | cereal | pepper | strawberry |
| butter | milk | salt | sugar |

1. ___*milk*___ carton   5. _____ shaker

2. _____ jam   6. _____ shaker

3. _____ knife   7. _____ bowl

4. _____ box   8. _____ table

6 Practice

Combine the word in capital letters with the words under it. You can put the word in front of or after the word in capital letters. Write the definition. Check your answers with your teacher or a dictionary.

1. PAPER

   hat _____

   towel _____

   wall _____

2. TV

   dinner _____

   tray _____

   color _____

3. CAR

   seat _____

   radio _____

   toy _____

4. COFFEE

   maker _____

   pot _____

   beans _____

5. CAMERA

   digital _____

   video _____

   case _____

6. CLOTHES

   hanger _____

   work _____

   rain _____

Adjectives and Adverbs

7. HISTORY

art   _____

class   _____

teacher _____

8. CAKE

birthday _____

rice   _____

plate   _____

9. HAND

hour   _____

shake   _____

ball   _____

10. NIGHT

time   _____

Saturday _____

light   _____

11. BOOK

note   _____

store   _____

match   _____

12. APPLE

juice   _____

pie   _____

sauce   _____

13. HOUSE

boat   _____

mate   _____

dog   _____

14. SALT

table _____

shaker _____

water _____

15. WATCH

wrist _____

digital _____

stop _____

16. TRUCK

driver _____

stop _____

garbage _____

17. SHOE

store _____

horse _____

sale _____

18. ROAD

work _____

block _____

dirt _____

19. COMPUTER

desk _____

screen _____

chip _____

20. PHONE

cell _____

book _____

number _____

13b Word Order of Adjectives

Student Book 1 p. 321, Student Book 1B p. 129

7 | Practice

Put the adjectives in the correct order.

1.	paper/brown	a/an	*brown paper*	bag
2.	black and white/old	a/an		TV
3.	plastic/cheap/white	a/an		toy
4.	blue/ugly/old	a/an		coat
5.	gray/cute/small	a/an		dog
6.	metal/dirty/cold	a/an		chair
7.	wooden/new/small	a/an		desk
8.	long/boring	a/an		exercise
9.	hot/delicious/chocolate	a/an		cookie
10.	small/clean/green	a/an		room

8 | Practice

Put the adjectives in the correct order.

1.	Italian/handsome/young	a/an		man
2.	brown/comfortable/leather	a/an		chair
3.	new/English/interesting	a/an		movie
4.	narrow/dangerous/short	a/an		street
5.	old/diamond/expensive	a/an		necklace
6.	Chinese/old/nice	a/an		woman
7.	Japanese/white/delicious	some		rice
8.	cold/sunny	a/an		morning
9.	cold/sweet	some		ice cream
10.	medium/red/good	a/an		apple

9 Practice

Complete the sentences with words from the list. Use each word once.

big	dining	nice	sunny
cheese	grocery	picnic	wooden

Fernando and Sylvia live in a _____ one-bedroom apartment. The bedroom
                                          1
is clean, and the living room is _____. In the _____ room, there is
                                          2   3
a _____ table with chairs. On the balcony, they have a _____ table.
              4   5
Their apartment is near the _____ store. Right now, Fernando is having a
                                      6
_____ sandwich. They have a _____ life.
          7   8

10 Practice

Use two adjectives or nouns used as adjectives to describe these things.

1. your room

   I have a small blue room _____.

2. your school

   _____.

3. your bicycle

   _____.

4. your hair

   _____.

5. your parents

   _____.

6. your shirt

   _____.

7. your computer

   _____.

8. your best friend

   _____.

9. your favorite vacation

   _____.

10. your backpack

_____ .

11. your wallet

_____ .

12. your city

_____ .

13c *The Same (As), Similar (To), and Different (From)*

Student Book 1 p. 324, Student Book 1B p. 132

11 Practice

Complete the sentences with *the same (as), similar (to),* or *different (from)*. Your answers may vary.

1. Life in the country is _____ life in the city.

2. Men are _____ women.

3. Fast food in the United States is _____ fast food in South America.

4. Teenagers in Japan are _____ teenagers in England.

5. Mothers everywhere are _____ .

6. Weather in Brazil and weather in Argentina are _____ .

7. Music from the 1960s is _____ music from 2000.

8. IBM computers and PCs are _____ .

9. Nine-year-old children and ten-year-old children are _____ .

10. People around the world are _____ .

12 Practice

Look at the photos. Then complete the sentences with *the same (as), similar (to),* or *different (from)*.

Photo A   **Photo B**

1. Photo A is _____ photo B.

2. Photos A and B are _____ .

Photo C

Photo D

Photo E

Photo F

3. Photo C is _____ photo D.

4. Photos C and D are _____.

5. Photo E is _____ photo F.

6. Photos E and F are _____.

13 Practice

Write about you and your family. Use *the same (as)*, *similar (to)*, or *different (from)*. Use the prompts or your own ideas.

1. have/eyes

    I have the same eyes as my dad _____.

2. enjoy/hobbies

    _____.

3. have/hair

    _____.

4. like/music

    _____.

5. be/height

    _____.

6. read/books

    _____.

13d *Like* and *Alike*

Student Book 1 p. 326, Student Book 1B p. 134

|14| Practice

Complete the sentences with *like* or *alike*.

1. Artie and Archie have similar names. Their names are _____*alike*_____.

2. Artie and Archie have similar houses. Artie's house is _____
   Archie's house.

3. Artie and Archie have similar hobbies. Artie's hobbies are _____
   Archie's hobbies.

4. Artie and Archie have similar eyes. Their eyes are _____.

5. Artie and Archie have similar gardens. Artie's garden is _____
   Archie's garden.

6. Artie and Archie went to similar universities. Artie's university is
   _____ Archie's university.

7. Artie and Archie have similar furniture. Arties' furniture is _____
   Archie's furniture.

8. Artie and Archie buy similar books. Artie's books are _____
   Archie's books.

9. Artie and Archie have similar hair. Their hair is _____.

10. Artie and Archie have similar digital cameras. Their cameras are

    _____.

11. Artie and Archie have similar TVs. Their TVs are _____.

12. Artie and Archie have similar children. Artie's children are _____
    Archie's children.

13. Artie and Archie bought similar computers. Artie's computer is
    _____ Archie's computer.

14. Artie and Archie have similar cell phones. Their cell phones are

    _____.

15. Artie and Archie have similar watches. Their watches are _____.

15 Practice

Which of these things are similar? Why? Use *like* or *alike* in your answers.

Austria	college	limes	shoes
cigarettes	cup	ocean	Switzerland
cigars	glass	sandals	university
clock	lemons	sea	watch

1. _Lemons are like limes._ (OR) _Lemons and limes are alike_ .
   They're both sour   .

2. _____ .

3. _____ .

4. _____ .

5. _____ .

6. _____ .

7. _____ .

8. _____ .

13e Comparative Form of Adjectives: *-er* and *More*

Student Book 1 p. 328, Student Book 1B p. 136

16 Practice

Write the comparative form of the adjectives.

1. short   _shorter than_   9. friendly   _____

2. slim   _____   10. old   _____

3. tall   _____   11. nice   _____

4. busy   _____   12. sweet   _____

5. good   _____   13. late   _____

6. heavy   _____   14. exciting   _____

7. early   _____   15. far   _____

8. handsome   _____   16. happy   _____

17 Practice

Write the comparative form of the adjectives.

1. warm _____
2. cool _____
3. interesting _____
4. loud _____
5. shy _____
6. large _____
7. rich _____
8. new _____

9. fast _____
10. modern _____
11. quiet _____
12. cheap _____
13. easy _____
14. bad _____
15. serious _____
16. delicious _____

18 Practice

Complete the sentences about the two restaurants. Use the comparative form of the adjectives in parentheses.

	Tom's Coffee Shack	Le Bon Mot
Dinner	$10 – $15	$25 – $40
Hours	10:00 A.M. – 9:30 P.M.	6:00 P.M. – 11:30 P.M.
Founded	1998	1972
Capacity	45 people	75 people
Food Rating	★★	★★★

1. Tom's Coffee Shack is (cheap) _____*cheaper than*_____ Le Bon Mot.

2. Le Bon Mot is (expensive) _____ Tom's Coffee Shack.

3. Tom's is open (early) _____ Le Bon Mot.

4. Le Bon Mot is open (late) _____ Tom's.

5. Tom's is (new) _____ Le Bon Mot.

6. Le Bon Mot is (big) _____ Tom's.

7. Tom's is (small) _____ Le Bon Mot.

8. Le Bon Mot is (old) _____ Tom's.

9. The food at Le Bon Mot is (good) _____ the food at Tom's Coffee Shack.

19 **Practice**

Complete the sentences about the two movies. Use the comparative form of the adjectives in parentheses. Some information is provided.

	Battle Guns from Space	Love Sweet Love
Length	120 minutes	90 minutes
Story	Three brothers fight an evil space monster.	A young man and woman fall in love.
Rating	★★★★	★★
Year	2003	2000

1. *Battle Guns from Space* is (long) _____ longer than _____ Love Sweet Love.

2. *Love Sweet Love* is (short) _____ Battle Guns from Space.

3. *Battle Guns from Space* is (good) _____ Love Sweet Love.

4. *Battle Guns from Space* is (exciting) _____ Love Sweet Love.

5. *Battle Guns from Space* is (interesting) _____ Love Sweet Love.

6. *Battle Guns from Space* is (new) _____ Love Sweet Love.

7. *Love Sweet Love* is (old) _____ Battle Guns from Space.

8. *Love Sweet Love* is (slow) _____ Battle Guns from Space

20 **Practice**

Complete the sentences about San Francisco and Tokyo. Use the comparative form of the adjectives in parentheses. Some information is provided.

San Francisco		**Tokyo**	
Population:	776,000	Population:	12,000,000
Average temperature:	40–70°F / 4–21°C	Average temperature:	30–85 F° / -1–29°C
Rain:	19.3 inches / 49 cm	Rain:	60 inches / 152 cm

1. Tokyo is (big) _____ bigger than _____ San Francisco.

2. San Francisco is (small) _____ Tokyo.

3. Tokyo is (crowded) _____ San Francisco.

4. Tokyo is (rainy) _____ San Francisco.

5. San Francisco is (warm) _____ Tokyo in the winter.

6. Tokyo is (cold) _____ San Francisco in the winter.

7. Tokyo is (hot) _____ San Francisco in the summer.

8. Tokyo is (expensive) _____ San Francisco.

9. Tokyo is (exciting) _____ San Francisco.

10. Tokyo is (old) _____ San Francisco.

21 Practice

Complete the sentences about Buenos Aires and Paris. Use the comparative form of the adjectives in parentheses. Some information is provided.

Buenos Aires		**Paris**	
Population:	12,400,000	Population:	2,000,000
Average temperature:	50–82°F / 5–29°C	Average temperature:	37–65°F / 3–18°C
Rain:	3.5 inches / 9 cm	Rain:	22 inches / 57 cm

1. Buenos Aires is (big) _____ Paris.

2. Paris is (rain) _____ Buenos Aires.

3. Buenos Aires is (warm) _____ Paris.

4. Paris is (far) _____ north _____

Buenos Aires.

5. Paris is (small) _____ Buenos Aires.

6. Buenos Aires is (dry) _____ Paris.

7. Paris is (cold) _____ Buenos Aires.

8. Buenos Aires is (far) _____ south

_____ Paris.

22 Practice

Write sentences about your life a year ago and now. Use comparative forms.

1. tall   *I'm taller now than I was a year ago* .

2. intelligent   _____

3. happy   _____

4. busy   _____

5. old   _____

6. thin/heavy   _____

7. shy/outgoing   _____

8. my hair/long OR short   _____

9. my classes/easy OR difficult   _____

10. my English/good OR bad _____

11. (your own idea) _____

12. (your own idea) _____

13f *As ... As, Not As ... As,* and *Less ... Than*

Student Book 1 p. 332, Student Book 1B p. 140

|23| Practice

Complete the sentences with *as ... as* and the adjectives in parentheses.

1. Shannon's school is (big) _____*as big as*_____ Renaldo's school.

2. Shannon's school is (fun) _____ Renaldo's school.

3. Shannon's school is (quiet) _____ Renaldo's school.

4. Shannon's school is (modern) _____

   Renaldo's school.

5. Shannon's teachers are (strict) _____

   Renaldo's teachers.

6. Shannon's school is (clean) _____ Renaldo's school.

7. Shannon's classes are (interesting) _____

   Renaldo's classes.

|24| Practice

Complete the sentences with *as ... as* or *not as ... as* and the adjectives in parentheses.

1. Her computer is (not, fast) _____ mine.

2. Her computer is (not, new) _____ mine.

3. Judy's computer is (expensive) _____ mine.

4. My computer is (not, large) _____ hers.

5. My computer is (not, heavy) _____ hers.

6. Her computer is (easy) _____ mine.

7. Her computer is (good) _____ mine.

Practice

Write the sentences to have the same meaning using *less*. Write "No change" if it isn't possible to use *less*.

1. Yoko's street isn't as safe as Joe's street. _No change_.

2. Joe's street isn't as dangerous as Yoko's.

   Joe's street is less dangerous than Yoko's.

3. Yoko's house isn't as comfortable as Joe's house.

   _____.

4. Yoko's house isn't as far away as Joe's house.

   _____.

5. Joe isn't as happy as Yoko.

   _____.

6. Joe isn't as outgoing as Yoko.

   _____.

7. Yoko isn't as shy as Joe.

   _____.

8. Joe isn't as nice as Yoko.

   _____.

9. Joe's job isn't as flexible as Yoko's job.

   _____.

10. Yoko's job isn't as difficult as Joe's job.

    _____.

11. Yoko's class isn't as early as Joe's class.

    _____.

12. Joe's class isn't as interesting as Yoko's class.

    _____.

13. Yoko isn't as serious as Joe.

    _____.

14. Joe's lunch isn't as delicious as Yoko's lunch.

    _____.

26 Practice

Many expressions use *as ... as*. Choose the word that best fits the expression. Use a dictionary if necessary.

1. Her daughter is as good as _____.   **a.** silk

2. What's wrong? You're as white as a _____.   **b.** honey

3. The little boy is as quiet as a _____.   **c.** gold

4. Your hand is as smooth as _____.   **d.** mouse

5. That cake is as sweet as _____.   **e.** ghost

27 Practice

Write *C* next to the expression if it is correct. Write *I* if the expression is incorrect. If the expression is incorrect, write the correct one.

_*I*_ **1.** He's as busy as a picture.   _He's as busy as a bee._

_____ **2.** She's as pretty as an ox.   _____

_____ **3.** That man is as strong as an ox.   _____

_____ **4.** I'm as hungry as a bear.   _____

_____ **5.** You're as cold as a beet.   _____

28 Practice

Write sentences with the same meaning using *as ... as*.

1. Vincenzo's Italian Restaurant is better than the Seaside Café.

    The Seaside Café isn't as good as Vincenzo's Italian Restaurant .

2. Vincenzo's Italian Restaurant is more expensive than the Seaside Café.

    _____.

3. The food at Vincenzo's Italian Restaurant is more delicious than the food at the

    Seaside Café. _____

    _____.

4. The Seaside Café is less luxurious than Vincenzo's Italian Restaurant.

    _____.

5. Vincenzo's Italian Restaurant is larger than the Seaside Café.

    _____.

6. The Seaside Café is dirtier than Vincenzo's Italian Restaurant.

_____.

7. Vincenzo's Italian Restaurant is newer than the Seaside Café.

_____.

8. Vincenzo's Italian Restaurant is fancier than the Seaside Café.

_____.

9. The music at the Seaside Café is louder than the music at Vincenzo's Italian

Restaurant. _____

_____.

10. The waiters at Vincenzo's Italian Restaurant are nicer than the waiters at the Seaside

Café. _____

_____.

29 Practice

Write sentences with the same meaning using _as ... as._

1. Amy's apartment is cheaper than Jeff's house.

   Jeff's house isn't as cheap as Amy's apartment .
   (OR)
   Amy's apartment isn't as expensive as Jeff's house .

2. Jeff's house is bigger than Amy's apartment.

_____.

3. Amy's apartment is less comfortable than Jeff's house.

_____.

4. Jeff's house is quieter than Amy's apartment.

_____.

5. Amy's apartment is safer than Jeff's house.

_____.

6. Jeff's house is farther from the school than Amy's apartment.

_____.

7. Amy's apartment is less modern than Jeff's house.

_____.

8. Jeff's house is cleaner than Amy's apartment.

_____.

9. Amy's apartment is older than Jeff's house.

_____.

13g Superlative Form of Adjectives: -*est* and *Most*
Student Book 1 p. 338, Student Book 1B p. 146

30 Practice
Write the superlative form of the adjectives.

1. short   *the shortest*   **9.** friendly _____

2. slim _____   **10.** old _____

3. tall _____   **11.** nice _____

4. busy _____   **12.** sweet _____

5. good _____   **13.** late _____

6. heavy _____   **14.** exciting _____

7. early _____   **15.** far _____

8. beautiful _____   **16.** happy _____

31 Practice
Write the superlative form of the adjectives.

1. warm _____   **9.** fast _____

2. cool _____   **10.** modern _____

3. difficult _____   **11.** quiet _____

4. loud _____   **12.** cheap _____

5. attractive _____   **13.** easy _____

6. large _____   **14.** bad _____

7. rich _____   **15.** serious _____

8. new _____   **16.** interesting _____

32 Practice

Complete the sentences with the correct form of the adjectives in parentheses.

1. Bristle cone pine tress are (old) _____*the oldest*_____ trees in the world.

2. Bee humming birds are (small) _____ birds in the world.

3. Siberian tigers are (large) _____ cats in the world.

4. The cheetah is (fast) _____ land animal in the world.

5. Blue whales are (big) _____ animals in the world.

6. Giraffes have (long) _____ necks of all animals.

7. The rhinoceros beetle is (strong) _____ animal in

   the world. It can carry 850 times its weight!

8. The lionfish is (beautiful) _____ fish in the sea.

33 Practice

Write sentences using the comparative or superlative and the information in the chart.

Robert	Clint	Buddy
5'9"	5'11"	6'1"
175 lbs	190 lbs	200 lbs
24 years old	32 years old	40 years old
very outgoing	not shy	shy
takes classes part time	works and goes to school	has part-time job
smokes	exercises three days a week	exercises five days a week
eats fast food		

busy	heavy	outgoing	shy	thin
healthy	old	short	tall	young

1. _Buddy is the tallest_____.

2. _Clint is taller than Robert_ _____.

3. _____.

4. _____.

5. _____.

6. _____.

7. _____.

8. _____.

9. _____.

10. _____.

11. _____.

12. _____.

13. _____.

14. _____.

15. _____.

34 Practice

Write answers to the following questions.

1. Who is the tallest person in your class?

_____.

2. Who is the most intelligent person in your school?

_____.

3. What is the most popular place in your town?

_____.

4. What is the best restaurant in your town?

_____.

5. What was the worst day of your life?

_____.

6. Who is the friendliest person you know?

_____.

7. What was the best day of your life?

_____.

8. Who is the funniest person in your family?

_____.

9. What was the most difficult class you had last year?

_____.

10. What's the tallest building in your town?

_____.

35 Practice

Write *C* next to the sentence if the superlative is used correctly. Write *I* if the superlative is used incorrectly. If the superlative is incorrect, write the correct one.

_____ **1.** Mt. Everest is the tallest mountain in the world.

_____ **2.** Gabriella was the most prettiest girl at the party.

_____ **3.** Sam's apartment is the most cheap.

_____ **4.** What was the most important day of your life?

_____ **5.** That's the best store in the mall.

_____ **6.** Todd lives the farest away.

_____ **7.** Valerie is the nicest person I know.

_____ **8.** Arturo gets up the most early.

1. _No change_ _____.

2. _Gabriella was the prettiest girl at the party_ _____.

3. _____.

4. _____.

5. _____.

6. _____.

7. _____.

8. _____.

13h *One Of The* + Superlative + Plural Noun

Student Book 1 p. 342, Student Book 1B p. 150

36 Practice

Write sentences using the *"one of the* + superlative + plural noun" pattern.

1. Sahara Desert/hot place/the earth

   The Sahara Desert is one of the hottest places on the earth.

2. Empire State Building/tall building/New York City

   _____.

3. The Amazon River/old river/the world

   _____.

4. Mexico City/crowded city/the world

   _____.

5. rice/important food/Asia

   _____.

6. *The Matrix*/popular film/ever

   _____.

7. chile peppers/spicy ingredient/a burrito

   _____.

8. The Great Wall of China/long wall/ever built

   _____.

9. ice cream/cold dessert/the menu

   _____.

10. The Eiffel Tower/famous structure/Europe

    _____.

Write questions and answers using the "*one of the* + superlative + plural noun" pattern.

1. tall/people/in your class

   Who is one of the tallest people in your class ?

   Jennifer is one of the tallest people in our class .

2. nice/people/in your class

   _____ ?

   _____ .

3. intelligent/people/you know

   _____ ?

   _____ .

4. famous/place/in your town

   _____ ?

   _____ .

5. good/restaurant/in your town

   _____ ?

   _____ .

6. great/musician/in jazz

   _____ ?

   _____ .

7. good/book/you have read

   _____ ?

   _____ .

8. tall/building/in your town

   _____ ?

   _____ .

9. interesting/subjects/in school

   _____ ?

   _____ .

10. famous/person/your country

_____?

_____.

11. expensive/thing/you have

_____?

_____.

12. happy/day/in your life

_____?

_____.

13. good/place/for teenagers/in your town

_____?

_____.

14. bad/movie/you saw last year

_____?

_____.

13i Adjectives and Adverbs

Student Book 1 p. 344, Student Book 1B p. 152

38 Practice

Write the words from the list in the correct columns.

bad	easily	hard	rainy	softly
clean	expensive	hardly	sad	sweetly
crowded	fast	interesting	salty	warmly
differently	fluently	late	small	well
dirty	good	quickly		

Adjective	Adverb	Adjective or Adverb
bad		

Underline the correct form of the adjective or adverb.

1. Carlos plays guitar (good / well).

2. He's a (good / well) guitar player.

3. His bedroom is (dirty / dirtily).

4. We did the homework (easy / easily).

5. The homework was (easy / easily).

6. I love you (deep / deeply).

7. It was (bad / badly) news.

8. She gave me the news (nice / nicely).

9. She speaks Spanish (beautiful / beautifully).

10. Her Spanish is (beautiful / beautifully).

11. That pizza was (salty / saltily).

12. Drive (careful / carefully).

13. This is a (heavy / heavily) book.

14. Yes, but it's (interesting / interestingly).

15. Kathy's kitchen is (modern / modernly).

16. My bed isn't (comfortable / comfortably).

17. I sleep (comfortable / comfortably).

18. We drank the lemonade (thirsty / thirstily).

19. We were (thirsty / thirstily).

20. Lauren answered the question (quiet / quietly).

21. She's a (quiet / quietly) person.

22. Those shoes were (cheap / cheaply).

23. It's (hot / hotly)!

24. Bernice is a (careful / carefully) driver.

40 Practice

Underline the correct form of the adjective or adverb.

1. The flowers are growing (fast / fastly).

2. We got to class (late / lately).

3. Our teacher wasn't (happy / happily).

4. Erin finished the race (easy / easily).

5. It was an (easy / easily) race.

6. Jason went home (sad / sadly).

7. He was (sad / sadly).

8. Donovan is (busy / busily).

9. They arrived home (safe / safely).

10. Their neighborhood isn't (safe / safely).

11. (Happy / Happily) birthday!

12. The party was a lot of (fun / funnily).

41 Practice

Write *C* next to the sentence if the adjective or adverb is used correctly. Write *I* if the adjective or adverb is used incorrectly.

_C_ 1. This is a good book!

_____ 2. David drives too slow.

_____ 3. Their parents arrived home early.

_____ 4. He cooks good.

_____ 5. Gabe speaks German fluently.

_____ 6. Hiro is a good tennis player.

_____ 7. This room is very clean.

_____ 8. I sing bad.

_____ 9. Nelson came in the room quiet.

42 Practice

Use adverbs to talk about how you do the following actions.

cook	draw	play sports	take photos
dance	drive	speak English	talk
do math	play piano	study	work

1. _I cook frequently_____.

2. _____.

3. _____.

4. _____.

5. _____ .

6. _____ .

7. _____ .

8. _____ .

9. _____ .

10. _____ .

11. _____ .

12. _____ .

13j Comparative and Superlative Forms of Adverbs

Student Book 1 p. 347, Student Book 1B p. 155

43 Practice

Complete the sentences using the comparative form of the underlined adverbs.

1. Kathy speaks English <u>fluently</u>, but Sue ____*speaks it more fluently*____ .

2. Kathy works <u>carefully</u>, but Sue _____ .

3. Sue drives <u>slowly</u>, but Kathy _____ .

4. Sue discusses politics <u>intelligently</u>, but Kathy _____ .

5. Kathy finished the test <u>quickly</u>, but Sue _____ .

6. Kathy plays piano <u>well</u>, but Sue _____ .

7. Sue speaks <u>politely</u> with customers, but Kathy _____ .

8. Kathy runs <u>fast</u>, but Sue _____ .

9. Sue did the job <u>easily</u>, but Kathy _____ .

10. Kathy gets to work <u>early</u>, but Sue _____ .

44 Practice

Write sentences using the comparative form of adverbs in the list or your own.

| beautifully | early | friendly | quickly |
| carefully | frequently | hard | well |

1. *Sharon paints beautifully, but Paco paints more beautifully.*

2. _____ .

3. _____ .

4. _____ .

5. _____ .

6. _____ .

7. _____ .

8. _____ .

45 Practice

Read the descriptions of three new cars. Use adjectives and adverbs from the list to write sentences with comparatives and superlatives.

big/small   clean/dirty   quickly/slowly   safe/dangerous
cheap/expensive   fast/slow   rough/smooth   well/bad

The Eco	The Tank	The Splendor
30 mi./gal	10 mi./gal	25 mi./gal
2 passengers	8 passengers	5 passengers
top speed: 75 mph	top speed: 60 mph	top speed: 100 mph
$10,000	$75,000	$45,000
good for the environment	bad for the air	causes a little air pollution
safety rating – ★★★	safety rating – ★★	safety rating – ★★★★★
handles well	hard to handle	handles okay
drives roughly	drives okay	drives smoothly

1. _The Eco handles the best_ _____ .

2. _____ .

3. _____ .

4. _____ .

5. _____ .

6. _____ .

7. _____ .

8. _____ .

9. _____ .

10. _____ .

13k As ... As with Adverbs

Student Book 1 p. 350, Student Book 1B p. 158

46 Practice

Write sentences using *as ... as* and information from the chart about Justin and Al.

Justin	Al
gets up at 5:50 A.M.	gets up at 9:00 A.M.
not good at sports	good at sports
works quickly	doesn't work quickly
doesn't speak French well	speaks French fluently
goes to bed at 11:00 P.M.	goes to bed at 3:00 A.M.
good cook	doesn't cook well
does well in school	doesn't do well in School

1. *Justin doesn't play sports as well as Al does* .

2. _____ .

3. _____ .

4. _____ .

5. _____ .

6. _____ .

7. _____ .

8. _____ .

9. _____ .

10. _____ .

11. _____ .

12. _____ .

47 Practice

Diane has a job interview tomorrow. Her father is giving her advice. Write sentences using *as ... as* + *you can*.

1. arrive/early

    Arrive as early as you can .

2. sleep/good/the night before

    _____ .

3. dress/neatly

_____.

4. answer the questions/well

_____.

5. listen to the questions/carefully

_____.

6. thank them/nicely

_____.

7. write a thank you note/soon

_____.

48 Practice

Write about events in your life using _as ... as_ + _could_.
Use adverbs from the list and your own.

carefully	hard	well
fast	quickly	

1. _Last year, I studied for my exams as hard as I could_ .

2. _____

_____.

3. _____

_____.

4. _____

_____.

5. _____

_____.

6. _____

_____.

7. _____

_____.

A **Choose the best answer, A, B, C, or D, to complete the sentence. Mark your answer by darkening the oval with the same letter.**

1. My mother has a _____ handbag.

   A. beautiful old red   Ⓐ Ⓑ Ⓒ Ⓓ
   B. old red beautiful
   C. red beautiful old
   D. beautiful red old

2. Jefferson finished the work _____.

   A. fastly   Ⓐ Ⓑ Ⓒ Ⓓ
   B. fast
   C. quick
   D. slow

3. Becky is _____ girl in the class.

   A. more intelligent   Ⓐ Ⓑ Ⓒ Ⓓ
   B. most intelligent
   C. the more intelligent
   D. the most intelligent

4. Janice's apartment is _____ mine.

   A. more cheaply   Ⓐ Ⓑ Ⓒ Ⓓ
   B. cheaper than
   C. more cheaper
   D. the cheapest than

5. Ann isn't _____ Sheila.

   A. the same than   Ⓐ Ⓑ Ⓒ Ⓓ
   B. as popular than
   C. as popular as
   D. different

6. Look at the _____ car.

   A. dirty blue old   Ⓐ Ⓑ Ⓒ Ⓓ
   B. old dirty blue
   C. old blue dirty
   D. dirty old blue

7. My sister's eyes are _____ my mother's.

   A. the same as   Ⓐ Ⓑ Ⓒ Ⓓ
   B. the same
   C. the same than
   D. same as

8. Joanne is _____ Katie.

   A. more heavy than   Ⓐ Ⓑ Ⓒ Ⓓ
   B. heavier than
   C. as heavier as
   D. heavy than

9. Joyce doesn't play piano _____ Irv.

   A. as good as   Ⓐ Ⓑ Ⓒ Ⓓ
   B. the best
   C. as well as
   D. better

10. Osaka is _____ in Japan.

    A. one of the   Ⓐ Ⓑ Ⓒ Ⓓ
       nicest cities
    B. nicer city than
    C. one of the nicest city
    D. one of the nicest

B **Find the underlined word or phrase, A, B, C, or D, that is incorrect. Mark your answer by darkening the oval with the same letter.**

1. Yellowstone <u>is the</u> <u>older</u> <u>national park</u>
             A   B   C

   <u>in the United States</u>.
          D

   Ⓐ Ⓑ Ⓒ Ⓓ

2. <u>Jason is</u> <u>alike</u> his brother John. <u>They are</u>
      A   B   C

   very <u>polite</u>.
       D

   Ⓐ Ⓑ Ⓒ Ⓓ

3. <u>Don't write</u> on the <u>white small</u>
      A   B

   <u>piece of paper</u> <u>on your desk</u>.
      C   D

   Ⓐ Ⓑ Ⓒ Ⓓ

4. <u>Yesterday</u> <u>was hot</u>, but today was
      A   B

   one of the <u>hottest day</u> <u>of the year</u>.
               C   D

   Ⓐ Ⓑ Ⓒ Ⓓ

5. <u>Our last house was</u> <u>more</u> <u>better</u> <u>than</u> the
         A   B   C   D

   one we live in now.

   Ⓐ Ⓑ Ⓒ Ⓓ

6. Rodney's town is similar <u>like</u> Gilberto's
                          A

   town, but <u>Gilberto's house is</u> <u>bigger than</u>
                 B   C

   <u>Rodney's</u>.
      D

   Ⓐ Ⓑ Ⓒ Ⓓ

7. <u>Therese finished</u> the race <u>more</u> <u>quick</u> <u>than</u>
      A   B   C

   the <u>other women</u>.
        D

   Ⓐ Ⓑ Ⓒ Ⓓ

8. <u>Life in the 1900s</u> <u>was very</u> <u>different</u> <u>than</u>
      A   B   C   D

   life today.

   Ⓐ Ⓑ Ⓒ Ⓓ

9. Please drive as <u>carefully</u> <u>than</u> <u>you can</u>.
                 A   B   C

   The traffic is <u>heavy</u> today.
                D

   Ⓐ Ⓑ Ⓒ Ⓓ

10. Eun Ji worked <u>as</u> <u>quick</u> as she <u>could</u>, but
                   A   B   C

    she <u>didn't finish</u> the test.
         D

    Ⓐ Ⓑ Ⓒ Ⓓ

UNIT 14
THE PRESENT PERFECT TENSE

14a The Present Perfect Tense of *Be: For* and *Since*

Student Book 1 p. 356, Student Book 1B p. 164

1 | Practice

Complete the sentences with the present perfect of the verb *be*. You may use contractions.

1. Mei came to this country six years ago. She

   <u>has been / 's been</u> here for six years.

2. Mei met Lin three years ago. They

   _____ friends for three years.

3. Mei and Lin moved into their apartment last August. They _____ in

   their apartment since August.

4. Mei became a nurse in 2003. She _____ a nurse since 2003.

5. Lin started school last September. She _____ a student since last

   September.

6. Lin caught a cold last Monday. She _____ sick since last Monday.

7. Mei started working a lot six weeks ago. She _____ very busy

   for six weeks.

8. Mei didn't eat breakfast this morning. She _____ hungry since

   this morning.

9. Lin met her boyfriend a year ago. She _____ with her boyfriend

   for a year.

10. Mei and Lin are happy. They _____ happy since they met each other.

2 Practice

Complete the sentences with the present perfect of the verb *be*. You may use contractions.

1. Gerald married Carol 25 years ago. They _'ve been / have been_ married for 25 years.

2. He became a doctor many years ago. He _____ a doctor for many years.

3. Carol quit her job last year. She (not) _____ at her job since last year.

4. Carol became interested in gardening 15 years ago. She _____

   interested in gardening for 15 years.

5. Carol was very sick last summer. She (not) _____ sick since

   last summer.

6. They moved to Hawaii last January. They _____ in Hawaii since

   last January.

7. Their daughter had a baby six months ago. They _____

   grandparents for six months.

8. Gerald and Carol started to build a new house last month. They

   _____ busy since last month.

3 Practice

Write *for* or *since* in the blanks.

1. ___since___ last week
2. ___for___ 30 minutes
3. _____ 1999
4. _____ one month
5. _____ five years
6. _____ 11:00
7. _____ Tuesday
8. _____ last Thursday
9. _____ two days
10. _____ January

11. _____ 2002
12. _____ two weeks
13. _____ last night
14. _____ half an hour
15. _____ 9:00 this morning
16. _____ midnight
17. _____ one year
18. _____ 15 weeks
19. _____ this afternoon
20. _____ a few months

4 Practice

Read the following information. Write sentences using the present perfect of the verb be.

1. Jose and Angela moved to Los Angeles in 2001.

   <u>*Jose and Angela have been*</u>

   <u>*in Los Angeles since 2001*</u> .

2. They had a baby in 2002.

   _____ .

3. Jose became interested in architecture five years ago.

   _____ .

4. Jose started school last year.

   _____ .

5. Angela became a bus driver a year and a half ago.

   _____ .

6. They moved in with Angela's parents a few months ago.

   _____ .

5 Practice

Complete the sentences with the present perfect of the verb be. Use ideas from the list or your own.

a good place to visit	busy	happy	sleeping well
an English student	famous	married	studying English

1. The singer Marc Anthony <u>*has been very famous*</u> for <u>*six years*</u> .

2. My country _____ for _____ .

3. My best friend _____ since _____ .

4. My best friend _____ for _____ .

5. I _____ since _____ .

6. My parents _____ for _____ .

7. My family _____ since _____ .

8. I _____ interested in _____

   since _____ .

9. I (not) _____ since _____ .

10. I (not) _____ for _____ .

14b The Present Perfect Tense: Regular and Irregular Verbs

Student Book 1 p. 361, Student Book 1B p. 169

6 Practice

Complete the chart with the correct forms of the verbs.

Base Form	Simple Past	Past Participle
1. *make*	*made*	*made*
2.	*had*	
3.	*wrote*	
4.		*spoken*
5. *read*		
6.	*called*	
7.		*studied*
8. *be*		
9.		*visited*
10.	*knew*	
11.		*gone*

7 Practice

Read about Laura and Tina. Then write sentences about the story using the present perfect tense.

Laura   **Tina**

Laura and Tina are sisters, but their lives are very different. They grew up in New York City and Laura lives there now. Laura went to college and graduated in 2000. She is a doctor. Laura got married last year. She and her husband Terry had a baby six months ago. They moved into their house last spring.

Tina did not go to college. She left New York after high school and went to Florida. She became a full-time artist when she moved to Florida. Tina started selling paintings six months ago, and now she is selling a lot of them. Tina and her two cats moved into their loft three years ago. The last time Tina saw Laura was nine years ago. Laura is going to visit Tina in Florida for the first time this fall.

The Present Perfect Tense

1. Laura/live/in New York all her life

   Laura has lived in New York all her life   .

2. Tina/live/Florida/high school

   _____ .

3. Laura/be/doctor/2000

   _____ .

4. Laura/be/married/last year

   _____ .

5. Tina/not see/Laura/nine years

   _____ .

6. Tina and her cats/live/loft/three years

   _____ .

7. Terry and Laura/be/parents/six months

   _____ .

8. They/live/house/last spring

   _____ .

9. Tina/work/artist/nine years

   _____ .

10. Tina/sell/paintings/six months

   _____ .

14c The Present Perfect Tense: Negative Statements and Questions

Student Book 1 p. 365, Student Book 1B p. 173

8 | Practice

Complete the questions and answers with the present perfect tense of the verbs in parentheses. You may use short answers.

1. A: (you, go) *Have you gone* to the store?

   B: No, I _____. I'll go now.

2. Henry (know) _____ Julia since they were children. They (be) _____ friends for a long time.

3. A: How long (have) _____ Susan _____ her dog?

B: She (have) _____ him for nine years.

4. A: I (not, write) _____ any email this morning.

B: Really? You _____?

A: Really. I (be) _____ very busy.

5. A: How long (own) _____ Mr. Travis _____ his store?

B: He (own) _____ it for 25 years.

A: How long (know) _____ you _____ him?

B: I (know) _____ him all my life! He's my grandfather.

6. A: (see) _____ you _____ my homework?

B: Yes, I _____. It's on the table.

7. A: (send) _____ you _____ the mail?

B: No, _____. I forgot. Sorry.

8. A: I'm hungry. (make) _____ you _____ lunch?

B: Yes, I _____.

9. A: How long (speak) _____ Peter _____ German?

B: I don't know. I know he (study) _____ it for many years.

10. A: How long (play) _____ your son _____ soccer?

B: He (play) _____ soccer for a year, but he (be) _____ more interested in tennis lately.

Practice

Complete the sentences with the present perfect tense of the verbs in parentheses. You may use short answers. Pay attention to the word order in questions.

A. An interviewer is talking to a famous singer.

Interviewer: How long (you, want) <u>have</u>

<u>you wanted</u> to be a singer?
                    1

Singer: I (know) _____
                            2

that I wanted to sing since I was

a child.

Interviewer: Now you are famous. (change)

_____
              3

this _____ your life?
              (3)

Singer: Yes, I (be) _____ lucky. I
                            4

(travel) _____ to many countries, and
                    5

I (have) _____ a very good time.
                    6

Interviewer: So what are you doing now?

Singer: Well, I (write) _____ some new songs, and I
                            7

(be) _____ very busy.
              8

B. Cho is talking to his English teacher.

Cho: How long (you, be) _____ an English teacher?
                                    1

David Brown: I (be) _____ a teacher for ten years.
                            2

Cho: How long (you, live) _____ in Korea?
                                    3

David Brown: We (be) _____ in Seoul for a few months. My
                            4

wife is from Korea. She (not, speak) _____
                                                    5

Korean since she was a young girl.

Cho: (you, visit) _____ other cities in Korea?
                            6

David Brown: Yes, we (travel) _____ to many places. We
                                    7

(be) _____ very happy.
              8

C. Betty is in another country but she's very lonely.

Gloria: (you, make) _____ friends here?

Betty: No, I _____.

Gloria: You should. (you, call) _____ your parents?

Betty: Yes, I _____, but they weren't home.

Gloria: (you, write) _____ your friends?

Betty: Yes, but they (not, write) _____ me back.

D. Luanne and Robert are on their first date.

Luanne: How long (you, live) _____

_____ here?

Richard: I (live) _____

here for five years. And you?

Luanne: I (live) _____

here for one year. How long (you, be)

_____ an artist?

Richard: I (study) _____

art for many years, but I (not, make)

_____ a lot of money as an artist yet.

14d The Present Perfect Tense: *Ever* and *Never*

Student Book 1 p. 368, Student Book 1B p. 176

10 Practice

Write *C* next to the sentence if *ever* or *never* is used correctly. Write *I* if *ever* or *never* is used incorrectly.

__*I*__ **1.** I've ever seen that movie.

_____ **2.** Will has never had a motorcycle.

_____ **3.** Have you ever been to Thailand?

_____ **4.** Carrie has ever worked for that company for eight years.

_____ **5.** Tim hasn't never gone to that store.

_____ **6.** How long have you ever been here?

_____ **7.** Has Alice ever written a book?

_____ **8.** She has never written a book.

_____ **9.** Has Hugo ever traveled to Venezuela?

_____ **10.** Joshua has ever made many friends here.

II Practice

Read the story about Fran. Then write questions and answers about Fran using *ever*, *never*, and the present perfect tense.

Fran has lived in Los Angeles her whole life. She has a big family and loves living in California. She has never been to another country, and she has lived in the same house for 20 years. She loves going to movies and art museums. She is a good cook. She sometimes makes dinner for her friends. Fran is a writer and she works at home. She has many friends.

1. Fran/live/a different town

Has Fran ever lived in a different town ?

No, she has never lived in a different town . (OR)

No, she hasn't .

2. Fran/be/another country

_____ ?

_____ .

3. Fran/live/another city

_____ ?

_____ .

4. Fran/write/anything

_____ ?

_____ .

5. Fran/make friends

_____ ?

_____ .

6. She/make/dinner for her friends

_____ ?

_____ .

7. She/go/the movie theater

_____ ?

_____ .

8. She/be/an art museum

_____ ?

_____ .

---

12 | ## Practice

Write questions and affirmative and negative answers. Use _ever_, _never_, and the present perfect tense.

1. you/make/pizza

Have you ever made pizza ?

Yes, I have. I make pizza every month . (OR)

No, I've never made a pizza .

2. you/see/movie in English

_____ ?

_____ .

3. you/be/on TV

_____ ?

_____ .

4. you/live/in another country

_____ ?

_____ .

5. you/fly/in a helicopter

_____?

_____.

6. you/ride/horses

_____?

_____.

7. your family/go on vacation/in Europe

_____?

_____.

8. you/color/your hair

_____?

_____.

9. your best friend/have/a party

_____?

_____.

10. you/be/very sick

_____?

_____.

11. you/have/a very bad day

_____?

_____.

12. you/drive/a truck

_____?

_____.

A **Choose the best answer, A, B, C, or D, to complete the sentence. Mark your answer by darkening the oval with the same letter.**

1. They have been friends _____ two years.

   A. since Ⓐ Ⓑ Ⓒ Ⓓ
   B. ever
   C. for
   D. never

2. Has Fernando _____ been to Mexico?

   A. since Ⓐ Ⓑ Ⓒ Ⓓ
   B. ever
   C. for
   D. never

3. Have you ever _____ to Egypt?

   A. goes Ⓐ Ⓑ Ⓒ Ⓓ
   B. went
   C. go
   D. gone

4. Liu has _____ been to Hawaii.

   A. since Ⓐ Ⓑ Ⓒ Ⓓ
   B. ever
   C. for
   D. never

5. Cheryl and Rigo have been married _____ May.

   A. since Ⓐ Ⓑ Ⓒ Ⓓ
   B. ever
   C. for
   D. never

6. I've never _____ a bigger car.

   A. haven't seen Ⓐ Ⓑ Ⓒ Ⓓ
   B. saw
   C. see
   D. seen

7. Kenichi has been a chemist _____ last year.

   A. since Ⓐ Ⓑ Ⓒ Ⓓ
   B. ever
   C. for
   D. never

8. How long have you _____ here?

   A. worked Ⓐ Ⓑ Ⓒ Ⓓ
   B. ever worked
   C. work
   D. never

9. Jasmine has been a teacher _____ many years.

   A. since Ⓐ Ⓑ Ⓒ Ⓓ
   B. ever
   C. for
   D. never

10. I haven't _____ Spanish for 15 years.

   A. never spoken Ⓐ Ⓑ Ⓒ Ⓓ
   B. spoke
   C. speak
   D. spoken

B   **Find the underlined word or phrase, A, B, C, or D, that is incorrect. Mark your answer by darkening the oval with the same letter.**

1. They <u>have live</u> in the apartment <u>for</u> only
      A   B   C

   <u>three weeks</u>.
       D

   Ⓐ Ⓑ Ⓒ Ⓓ

2. Diego has <u>ever</u> <u>studied</u> English <u>since</u>
          A   B   C

   <u>he was</u> a high school student.
     D

   Ⓐ Ⓑ Ⓒ Ⓓ

3. He <u>has owned</u> <u>the store</u> <u>since</u> 22 years.
    A   B   C   D

   Ⓐ Ⓑ Ⓒ Ⓓ

4. <u>How long</u> <u>has you</u> <u>been</u> a
      A   B   C

   <u>computer programmer</u>?
        D

   Ⓐ Ⓑ Ⓒ Ⓓ

5. My parents <u>have</u> <u>ever</u> <u>been</u> to Paris. They
            A   B   C

   <u>loved</u> it.
     D

   Ⓐ Ⓑ Ⓒ Ⓓ

6. <u>Paul and Andrea</u> <u>have</u> <u>never</u> <u>went</u>
        A   B   C   D

   to India.

   Ⓐ Ⓑ Ⓒ Ⓓ

7. <u>How long</u> <u>has your mother</u> <u>ever</u> <u>worked</u> for
      A   B   C   D

   that company?

   Ⓐ Ⓑ Ⓒ Ⓓ

8. Yumiko hasn't <u>never</u> <u>worked</u> for that
                A   B

   company <u>since</u> <u>1999</u>.
          C   D

   Ⓐ Ⓑ Ⓒ Ⓓ

9. Chuck <u>has</u> <u>been</u> at school <u>for</u> 9:00
         A   B   C

   <u>this morning</u>.
      D

   Ⓐ Ⓑ Ⓒ Ⓓ

10. Young Ji hasn't <u>never</u> <u>been</u> home <u>since</u>
                 A   B   C

    <u>last Saturday</u>.
       D

    Ⓐ Ⓑ Ⓒ Ⓓ